A Bird in the Hand
And a Bear in the Bush

A Halfway House for Wildlife

by Judy Hughes

 Chronicle Books

To Larry and Stephanie,
my loving accomplices and wonderful husband and daughter

Photographs on pages 10, 37, 49, 62, 107, 112, 118 taken by
Larry Hughes, all others by the author.

Library of Congress Cataloging in Publication Data
    A bird in the hand & a bear in the bush.

Hughes, Judy.

    1.   Wildlife rescue—Oregon.   I.   Title.
QL83.2.H83   637'.97'909795   75–46564
ISBN 0–87701–078–1

Chronicle Books
870 Market Street
San Francisco, Ca. 94102

Contents

ONE

Our Foster Home for Wildlife

Is it crazy to pamper two life styles at the same time? I mean, do you know anyone who gets up at 5 A.M. every day to battle fifty-five miles of dark and narrow winding road through rain, hail, snow, wind, and gravel to work all day at a professional city job, then, bleary-eyed, repeats the drive, returning home to the same gaping mouths that were stuffed before leaving in the morning? A large family? If you consider that at any one time we fed one dog, three cats, four horses, two ponies, ten cows with calves, a fluctuating assortment of shore birds, raccoons, deer, fox, owls, bear, and parakeet, you have some idea of the monumental task that awaited me. A husband and child shrieked equally for groceries.

Truthfully, I must admit at the outset that my husband drove both ways. Larry and I have a partnership marriage, although I'm not ashamed to say I blackmailed him—he either drove home or did the dishes.

We lived on a 175-acre ranch in the Coast Range of Western Oregon. Because national forest completely surrounded us in an isolated area, we ran our own little world—Larry, our daughter, Stephanie, and the ever-changing menagerie.

Another permanent member of the family was Heidi, our 100-pound German shepherd, who was an integral part of our wildlife work. All orphans received her special attention. We did the feeding, but Heidi did the cleaning—licking them from head to toe, even stimulating their bowels! Whether fawn, raccoon, fox, or bear, she added the extra solace a lonely orphan bawled for. She also demonstrated a natural instinct for assuming guardianship of the underling. When the fox vixen thought kitten tails were to pull, Heidi stepped in-between;

and if a pleading whine wouldn't work, she growled the fox away. In turn, when the cat pounced at the parakeet cage, Heidi scolded the cat. After several nasty spills from my green-broke mare, the dog decided I shouldn't ride that horse again. She circled and whined until I changed horses for an older, slower, safer mount.

It was uncanny what Heidi knew!

When Larry and I were first married, the accumulation of dog hair that gathered in his pants and blew in his face drove him mad. Ten years later, he's the one to suggest the bedroom for a dying fawn. He has learned that cleanliness is not next to godliness—compassion is. This does not suggest we live in a pigpen, although since Spook, the screech owl, died, I haven't the heart to clean his stain from the living-room lampshade. Turned toward the wall, who knows? Actually our velvet furniture and wall-to-wall carpet remained in remarkable condition, eliciting amazed looks from visitors no doubt expecting the worst.

We frown upon keeping wild animals as pets. Their heritage is freedom to enjoy a natural life. Too many people think it would be fun to own a raccoon, fox, or other wild animal, only to be upset later by poor adjustments. The truth is that raccoons turn on faucets, play in toilets, open cupboards, climb curtains, pillage cookie jars, and leave smelly deposits. Foxes are never housebroken and easily revert to the wild state when grown. Besides, a cage and human company simply don't predicate a happy life.

The animals we take in need help. They are orphaned, injured, or somebody's former pets. We give them temporary shelter and food, patch them up, and retrain them to independence. Some return to visit, some don't. The animals come to us from humane societies, veterinarians, state game officials, or individuals. We receive no financial help from any source. Our payment comes from seeing an injured bird heal, then soar to freedom . . . from showing a creek to a raccoon for the first time . . . from watching a fawn bewitch Heidi. Why us? Because we were needed.

From my observations of several agencies I have found that the state and federal wildlife departments that should be conducting this type of program are negligent. They treat animals as a crop or target. They are game managers, controlling wildlife for the hunter's harvest of the innocent. Thus, they are incapable of suddenly assuming the role of wildlife protector. Hence, the injured fawn requiring more attention will be "hit over the head." Fox and coyote orphans are routinely slaughtered because they are predators.

Federal and state regulations prevent most people from running an "orphanage," and reasonably so. Inadequate care, dirty cages, or failure to release the animals properly can do more harm than good. Government authorities granted us special permission, and in some cases issued the necessary licenses. We demonstrated the ability to care for animals in a professional manner. Our cages, pens, and facilities passed formal review and our background and prior experience as veterinary assistants and ranchers met with official approval. The remoteness of our ranch, combined with our willingness to do without vacations, entertainment, or new clothes and to drop large amounts of our budget on wildlife care, was also an unusual combination.

The mundane part of our life is the 8:00-to-5:00 routine that pays the bills. The first half of our life together was spent putting Larry through school. He has a B.A. in physics and a Master's in Business Administration. Then, giving up higher-salaried opportunities, we decided that the elation of owning enough land to protect wildlife, other than gophers, more than made up for monetary loss. We also prefer the wildlife jungle to the asphalt jungle for raising our daughter.

For Larry that means lengthy hours of work at the university. I'm somewhat luckier. I manage my own insurance business.

Truthfully, I'm not turned on by insurance, but it allows me to run my own office. This is very important, considering I often share the back room with a four-legged fugitive. Prospective clients are apt to hear moaning, scratching, crying, or barking. Through all this I manage to explore insurance possibilities with surprising *savoir-faire*.

Another advantage of being my own boss is the time element. For example, if someone shrieks into the phone for me to rescue a trapped owl, I'll slap a CLOSED sign on the door and race 100 miles to pick it up. A hurt owl can't wait. A potential client can. Because of this attitude I don't set insurance sales records, but I'm happy doing my own thing.

When Larry and I moved to the country, we had no intention of dropping out. I appreciate material things too much for that. In fact, the second look at our potential home had me close to tears.

"I thought it had siding. Why does it look so unfinished?" I asked.

"That's just tar paper, but look at the cracks."

"The kitchen is just a lean-to."

"Oh God, what have we done?"

Larry and I enjoy redoing old houses, but this was ridiculous. A week earlier when we made our deposit for the place, the creeks tumbling through rolling pastures surrounded by mountainous forest had entranced us. We didn't really look at the house.

"Maybe we should live in town and just keep the land until we can afford to build on it," Larry suggested.

"If we don't live on it, we may as well not have it. Besides, I want to be part of it, not just a visitor. We should also make sure we like living out there before building."

Unconvincingly nodding his head up and down, my worried husband agreed. "A mobile home! That's the answer!" he exclaimed while scanning the classified section of the newspaper.

"Hey, that sounds pretty good," I agreed. With moving day approaching and a minimum budget, that turned into the ideal solution. Literally hundreds of mobile-home models complicated the final decision. But when we first stepped inside the right model, we knew we had found our new home. The two-tone olive green combination gave us a cheerful feeling at first glance. Twelve feet wide by sixty-five feet long, with a living room that tipped out an additional few feet, it was the largest unit deliverable on that narrow road. There were two large bedrooms at each end and two bathrooms. Our worn-out blue furniture didn't match the green carpeting, so we splurged on a new living-room set. After all, the move was going to be comfortable. I couldn't guess how much more comfortable until we actually moved in.

Instant warmth at my finger tips! For years in our old house three wood stoves were our main heating source. To travel twenty-five stairs (and back) to the bathroom in the middle of the night was to be avoided at all costs. Our sex life improved, just to keep warm.

Worn out from working at the office, I would return home to a freezing house each day with a tired toddler. Because I worked only part time, it was my job to get the fires started, feed the horses, raccoons, and foxes, clean stalls, and bottle-feed twenty baby calves before starting dinner. That meant changing from career woman to ranch hand, from typewriter to manure shovel, from Chanel #5 to diapers. Between dumping the manure and reloading the wheelbarrow with clean bedding, I had to run into the house to stoke the fire, check Stephanie, and fill another batch of calf bottles. Larry conned me into thinking I had the better deal, since he worked full time. I've learned a lot since then.

We sold the calves when we moved to the larger ranch. I'm not sorry, though it was a heady feeling to have a herd of calves think of me as mother. We couldn't devote the necessary time to the babies, so we started over with a herd of yearlings instead. Heifers feed themselves.

A diverse acreage surrounded by timbered hills, our new ranch included marshland, beaver ponds, orchards, second-growth timber, fertile bottomland, and one island. It also boasted two different creeks. One ran the entire mile and a half length of our place. Although called a creek, in winter the stream became our own miniature Niagara, complete with rapids.

Our mobile home perched on a hill overlooking four different views. From the living-room window we exchanged friendly stares with elk, deer, coyote, and bear. With seventy inches of rain a year, the view from the window was important. Proud of a property that encompassed all our dreams, we called it Bear Creek Ranch. We even paid a signmaker to inscribe it in fifteen-inch letters.

What a drive to town! But Larry would drive through blizzards to get to work. When we first decided to move out so far, he took a lot of flack from co-workers who predicted the fifty-mile drive would cause high absenteeism in bad weather. So to keep from hearing "I told you so," we just got up earlier during snowstorms, mudslides, and high water.

Driving home, we listened to the helicopter traffic reports from San Francisco's KGO radio station, a thousand miles away. When we heard about the bumper-to-bumper tie-ups, we were content to be crunching along through our magnificent isolation. The everchanging beauty of the river by day-

The property that encompassed all our dreams.

light, with an occasional glimpse of an elk herd, was compensation for the dark winter months.

Living so far from the nearest doctor or veterinarian did at first concern me. But we had been living only ten miles from a hospital when I broke my elbow in a fall from that same worthless mare Heidi tried to warn me about, and I spent more time in the hospital waiting room, painfully filling out forms, than the longer drive would have taken. Besides, in a real emergency we could have used an air ambulance service organized on the coast.

We did a lot of our own veterinary work. Although we never had a doctor out, the veterinarian came twice. At ninety dollars a trip it had to be bad.

As for the neighbors, most of them would have resented any outsider moving into the area, but they disliked us because of our NO TRESPASSING and NO HUNTING signs. It was obvious our place had been a favorite hunting ground. We are both appalled by the love of killing that masquerades as sportsmanship. I'm not against eating meat—yet, but the "killing for fun" syndrome associated with hunting turns me off.

The same excuses for hunting are routinely given: the high price of meat, the eternal struggle of man against nature, the regulation of deer herds to avoid starvation, and enjoyment of the great outdoors. Whereas, it's a fact that getting outfitted for hunting is more expensive than buying meat. What sportsmanship is there in arming oneself with a high-caliber weapon to track down and shoot a defenseless animal? What sportsmanship is there in having trained hounds tree a bear or raccoon, to be killed by "the great white hunter?"

In areas with an oversupply of deer, man is responsible by eliminating predators and building up an unnatural abundance of deer in order to create an unlimited supply of living targets. Predators, starvation, and natural death would eliminate the weaker animals, rather than the hearty specimens that hunters kill. Another major factor in the starvation of deer is man's mismanagement of natural resources. The extensive overgrazing of sheep ruins the soil and depletes the deer's food supply. If you need an excuse to enjoy the great outdoors, do it with a camera. Stalking with a camera is more satisfying and requires more skill than hunting.

TWO

Always Room for One More Raccoon

Raccoons have been our most numerous guests. Intelligent and interesting animals, they are becoming popular pets, although they aren't really suited to confinement. If you live in the country and enjoy raccoons, it's more satisfying to put out food for the wild ones than to take freedom from a tame one.

The majority of raccoons we've hosted were from people who either grew tired of their unusual pet or suddenly had a tame pet turn "mean." Usually the cause of this aggression is unhappiness, frustration at being caged, and inability to breed. An intelligent animal like the raccoon needs more attention than most people are able to give. During estrous, an adult's normal urge is to mate.

Tame raccoons can make the adjustment to freedom again much more easily than most wild animals. In fact, their adaptability and versatility have enabled them to survive in populated areas. Omnivorous eaters, city raccoons turn to rummaging garbage cans for food. The most important factor in releasing tame raccoons is to free them in protected areas, so that they are less likely to get in trouble with a farmer or be seen too frequently by the wrong people. Because they have lost their fear of man, they are more susceptible to death by the trigger-happy than by starvation.

One day Nancy Cole, a new friend of mine, telephoned. "Judy, what am I gonna do with our raccoon? The neighbors are going crazy. He climbs through their car windows and tears the upholstery, and the other day he nipped the kid down the street. Pretty soon someone's sure to shoot him."

"Well, why don't you bring him over here? There's always

room for one more at our place," I answered. We fed wild coons, and Larry was overjoyed to have one he could actually touch.

The Coles tearfully brought their engaging pet. Although he was tame to them, he was thoroughly frightened by the car ride and new surroundings. Bolting from the car as quickly as the door opened, Bobby Coon loped from sight immediately. We really hadn't thought of a procedure for releasing our first wild client. We just wanted him to have a nodding acquaintance with us, meet the dogs, and know the feeding area before taking to the woods. The Cole family called his name as they searched the woods. Heidi's nose finally led us to a fir tree; and there, looking down from a height of four feet, was a very bewildered raccoon.

The Coles reluctantly left. It took several hours for curiosity to overcome Bobby's fear. To alleviate his panic, I locked up the dogs. Slowly he inched downward, then followed us to the barn for temporary confinement.

"Judy, get out here fast," Larry shouted the next morning, waking me from a sound sleep.

The inside of the tackroom was unrecognizable. Medicine and mineral oil dripped from the cabinets. Books were torn from shelves and thrown everywhere.

"Look at my movie film. It's ruined!" Larry yelled, eyeing hundreds of feet of unwound cellophane draped across mounds of wasted grain.

"My curtains are in shreds," I shrieked, lamenting precious hours spent creating them.

An icing of pillow feathers lent a festive air to the incident. Innocently sleeping amid the debris, Bobby Coon looked up and yawned.

"I thought these things only happened in Walt Disney movies," Larry remarked, as we laughed hysterically. Bobby Coon, having made his point, earned his immediate freedom.

"Do you think Bobby will get along with the dogs?" I asked as the two shepherds approached him. One of Heidi's nearly grown pups was still living with us and I wasn't sure what would happen.

As Cindy, the pup, lowered her head to sniff this stranger, Bobby's two arms went around her neck and he pulled her off balance. Closely entwined, they rolled down the bank to-

Jenny waits for a cookie.

gether. "Are they fighting? What's happening?" I called, as we ran down the incline with a worried Heidi.

The raccoon still had Cindy by the neck, nibbling her fur. But Cindy seemed to enjoy it and was wagging her tail and licking the raccoon's saucy little face. Viewing Heidi for the first time, he deserted Cindy to pull Heidi's tail. The dogs were both amazed at this unusual creature's brassiness. They danced around him.

We learned from experience that if raccoons grow up around dogs, they usually accept a strange dog without fear as an adult. However, lacking early friendships, they won't make that adjustment when mature. Bobby Coon had been raised with several large dogs and had thoroughly enjoyed romping with them, so he easily transferred his affection to our shepherds.

We allowed the raccoon visitation privileges in the house . . . but with limitations. Larry offered Bobby a graham cracker, then replaced the box in the kitchen cupboard. After carefully eating every crumb, Bobby got down from the sofa, opened the cupboard door, took another cracker, and returned the box. Intelligent enough to help himself, Bobby couldn't be restrained from getting his own thereafter.

Proceeding into Stephanie's room, the raccoon sniffed her

potty chair. As we watched him, our mouths fell open. "Do you see that?" we asked each other incredulously. "He used it!" After repeated attempts, Stephanie hadn't yet learned to use it—and she was bright for a toddler.

Because Larry was raised in the backwoods of Arkansas, country life wasn't new to him. Although poor, he had his own pony at an early age. As an adult, he didn't suffer a burning desire for a horse until I changed his mind. Some of our first dates were spent at riding stables. The first time I attempted to show off my equestrian ability, I fell flat on my face. My horse rounded a corner. I didn't. But that event didn't prevent me from nagging Larry for a horse of my own. So we acquired Nosegay (a name I loathe and can assure you I didn't choose). My gray beauty is the spoiled, spirited half Arabian that's tossed me a few times. But she seems to grin and always waits for me to try again. I love that crazy horse. In the saddle she bosses me around, even though she's as tame as a pup when I'm walking. Gay did do one worthwhile thing in her life. She foaled Duprey's Firebrand (a name I did choose). Immediately after Gay had given birth to her whiskey-colored filly, she was unusually protective, allowing no one but Larry or me to enter the pasture.

Bobby Coon was unconcernedly strolling across her pasture. He didn't see the enraged mare galloping after him.

"Get the coon! Get the coon!" I screamed to Larry at the top of my lungs.

Jumping the fence in one leap, Larry threw his waving arms up at the horse. "Shoo, get away. Get out of here!" he yelled, chasing Gay until the raccoon finally noticed the commotion and took off at full speed. Gay finally got over her extreme protectiveness and even endured the raccoon's overtures of friendship. As Bobby's little hands patted and rubbed Gay's legs a week later, she tolerated him with an indifferent glance.

Bobby never bit hard while playing, but, nevertheless, was too rough for Stephanie. Larry was his favorite, and the raccoon could usually be found riding my husband's shoulder, nibbling an ear or fingering shaggy hair. Larry spent many hours exploring the forest with Bobby Coon.

The creek was a delight to a raccoon accustomed to bathing in a bathtub. His nimble fingers were constantly feeling pebbles and turning over rocks searching for crawfish. Besides grubbing most of his own food, Bobby shared dry dog food with the shepherds. When mating season came, he craved company of his own kind and stayed away for longer and longer periods. Finally he returned no more, but he had hooked us on raccoons.

Paying $30 for a raccoon goes against my better judgment, but watching three children setting off firecrackers over a tiny, caged baby raccoon made the exorbitant price the lesser of two evils. I don't like to perpetuate the selling of baby raccoons, but it seemed the quickest way to rescue this one. She was so young that she should have been tamable. But the trauma brought about by the children's extreme abuse made her wilder than if she'd never been handled. Larry, Stephanie, and I gathered excitedly around the traveling cage, hoping to cuddle Jenny. As I opened the cage door, she growled and attacked my gloved hand. Even though she had only baby teeth, they were needle sharp. Too tiny to turn loose, she needed to be calmed and assured that we meant no harm.

"I'll be in the bathroom the rest of the night," I announced to the family. That seemed the best place to become acquainted. While wearing gloves, I tried to hold her against her will. As she fought against me by biting and growling, I calmly struggled to hold her to me. It seemed like a good idea at the time, this same treatment having tamed Duprey's Firebrand as a young filly. Newborn foals are afraid of people and battle to get loose, but if you calmly keep your arms around them, they eventually accept you and from that point on are tame. This reasoning didn't work with Jenny.

Two fruitless days later she seemed to dislike me even more. Perhaps the will of a wild animal is not so easily bent. Tossing the gloves aside, I was surprised to learn that Jenny had less fear of my bare hand and readily accepted food and stroking from me. Obviously the first owner had worn gloves, which she associated with pain.

Nightly I sat in the bathroom reading, pretending to ignore her as she became curious about me. Fingering my hair, ears, and hands, Jenny actually wanted to play with me. However, if I pressed the friendship or carried her to the large outdoor cage, she snapped angrily at me. So as not to carry her back and forth unnecessarily, I climbed into the cage with her. An unusually clean animal, Jenny preferred to wet and stool in water, so her cage was very easy to clean. One tub was for drinking, another for toilet.

I mistakenly gave Jenny temporary freedom before turning her loose permanently. Usually happy in her cage, she was now frustrated to land back in jail after the thrill of discovering puddles and apple trees. I could read the longing in her eyes as she paced nervously back and forth in her cage until I gave in and released her permanently.

Our six mallard ducks lived near Jenny's cage. Raised in the family bathtub from tiny fuzzy balls of fluff, they were our favorite creatures. Full of personality, they walked in formation and quacked in unison. Besides chasing the cats and dogs, they pulled the horse's tail and nipped the cats. Overly tame, they preferred the driveway to the creek. After enticing them to follow us to the creek, we sneaked away, leaving them to splash in the water. Quack! quack! quack! Right behind us. They preferred the gravel bed to a water bed.

Jenny was curious about the ducks, but they seemed to intimidate her. I didn't worry about them.

Quack! quack! quack! The ducks, unusually noisy one evening, brought me rushing outside from my warm bed. The moonlight count showed five ducks instead of six, and Jenny innocently sitting on top of the telephone pole. Searching frantically by flashlight, I finally located the sixth duck, bleeding from the beak and hiding in the weeds. She was in shock and allowed me to carry her inside. After a peaceful night, she recovered. However, there seemed to be no solution that night for the remaining ducks. They were frightened and wouldn't let me get close to them. Jenny couldn't be bribed back into her cage, even for grapes. As she was still so young, I didn't think it would be possible yet for her to kill a duck.

"In the morning when the ducks are quiet I'll pen them and think of something," I told Larry as we prepared for sleep. Periodic checking through the night showed Jenny still up the pole and the ducks all quiet.

But one duck didn't make it. Only the head and stomach eaten, the rest lay at the bottom of the utility pole. We wondered why the usually fearless ducks had run from Jenny. Why didn't they chase and nip her as they did the cats? I was angry to lose a duck this way, but not at Jenny, who was born to eat anything she could find. My frustrated feelings were momentarily directed against the instinct that allows animals to eat one another. Not able to change that, I could at least be the controlling power here and save the remaining ducks. We freed them at the city park, where they joined a protected flock and quacked happily out of sight.

Afraid of recapture, Jenny continued to avoid the cage. She gnawed on the duck carcass for several days and ate dry dog food I put out for her. Jenny climbed the fir tree in the back yard by entering Heidi's fenced area at night when the dog was inside the trailer. Jenny refused to come back down when she became aware of Heidi's proximity. Even when I removed Heidi from the area, she refused to believe the ground area in the yard was safe. Climbing and examining every minute detail, she made it "her" tree. She even changed her toilet habits, no longer using tubs of water but instead far-out branches of the tree. Look out below!

Several days later, she still hadn't left the tree, eating and drinking only small quantities of what I offered. Becoming convinced she wouldn't leave the tree via the yard, I nailed a one-by-four, twenty-five feet long, from the garage roof to the tree trunk. The narrow walkway proved to be exactly what the raccoon had been waiting for. Running excitedly across it, ten feet above the dog, Jenny used it immediately. Although the tree was still home, she now felt free to explore the surrounding creek and forest. Preferring to leave during the dark of night, she became a solitary explorer. The days were spent sleeping or watching us in the yard below. Preferring to keep dry, she was more likely to sleep through heavy rains and explore on clear evenings. Whenever the temperature dropped much below 30°, she remained in her warm nest box.

"Jenny!" I called every time I saw her peeking out from her quarters. She came quickly to the feeding station to visit with me. As I stood on the redwood picnic table, she allowed me to pet her while she sniffed my face and explored my hair. Although tame enough to chat with, she would not let us hold her.

After finding roundworms in her stool, I bought some worm-

Jenny spent her first weeks of freedom watching the commotion below her backyard fir tree.

ing medicine from the veterinarian, crushed the pill in peanut butter, and spread it on a graham cracker. Jenny took a big bite of her favorite food, then coughing and choking she tried to spit it out. It must have tasted awful, but she swallowed enough to attack the worms.

Her visits became less frequent as she gained more confidence in her own ability to survive. I worried when she was gone for two weeks in February, although it was breeding season. Maybe she had found a mate. Up to that time, Jenny had never left the tree or the food supply longer than a day, so I suspected she had mated or been hurt. Male raccoons are not mature enough to breed until their second year, but the females have about a sixty per cent chance of doing so.

As Larry and I played cards for a penny a point, I often glanced out the window hoping to see Jenny return to the tree. I was way behind.

"She's back!" I shouted, more than ready to terminate my rotten hand, and rushed out in the downpour to welcome Jenny. Her over-all appearance was rough and skinny. Fur was missing from her head and tail. However, licking my fingers as she reached for a graham cracker, she seemed as friendly as ever. Checking her nipples as she stood on her hind legs eating, I found no indications of babies that year.

Public pressure was responsible for closing a small municipal zoo in a nearby town. The cages were tiny, cement squares that barely left room for dreaming. We wanted to transport and release all the animals at our place, but somehow, with all the red tape involved, we ended with raccoons only. They had been returned to their former owner whose plan was to free them in his city yard. Then he heard about us. While taking delivery of the raccoons, I expected some kind of an animal lover, but was quickly disenchanted.

"I'm quite a coon hunter, you know. Got me several good coon hounds. I've killed me aplenty," he said.

"How can you kill the raccoons after you've had them as pets?" I asked.

"Aw, its awful easy. I work both sides of the fence." He went on to detail how he kills nursing raccoon mothers, confiscates their babies, and sells them to animal lovers—all completely legal.

The two raccoons snapped and growled while waiting for us in the traveling cage. Two hounds pawed and drooled expectantly over the captives. The masked pair became panic-stricken as saliva from the yipping dogs dripped onto their fur. It was hard to control my temper until I had the raccoons safely in the car.

We were pleased that the male and female, who had been cage mates for two years, would associate in the wild. Opening the cage at the base of the back-yard feeding station, we had decided Jenny's tree would be the best starting point. Then, aware of a plentiful food supply, they could explore the surrounding area as they grew braver.

Four days later they had not left the tree. Confiscating Jenny's box, they were lucky she stayed away for days at a time. Peeking at us in the yard below, they hesitated to come down to eat until dark. Timidly scampering across the garage roof at midnight, they expanded their territory on the fifth day.

As they learned that the inhabitants below weren't going to bother them, they stayed at the feeding area while I approached with graham crackers. The larger one, old Scar-Face, took the cracker and continued holding my hand, sniffing and feeling it as his eyes watched me closely. Somewhat bolder than the female, he barely nipped my finger. Satisfied when I didn't do anything, he let me stroke his head. I had no intentions of taming them further.

Loud growling outside brought me rushing with my flashlight. Jenny had returned for her share of the dog food. The new male was willing to share the wealth, but the female wanted no part of this interloper. With Jenny kept at bay on the garage roof, the piercing, trilling scream resumed. Grabbing a ladder, I offered food to the frightened Jenny. Not understanding why her tree now housed strangers, Jenny left without eating. Upset that my Jenny had been scared away by the larger city park raccoon, I hoped she would return.

Next morning I made a separate covered feeding station on the garage roof while Larry made another escape route from the feeding platform on the tree. He secured a twenty-foot alder tree from branch to ground outside the fenced yard. Beavers had felled the tree earlier. Now if Jenny returned, she would not be trapped on the tree and there would be space and food for all.

Several nights in a row, flashlight in hand, I watched for Jenny's return. Luckily she wasn't ready to forsake her handouts that easily; consequently she returned to tolerate the growls of the city park raccoons. As I offered favorite treats, all three animals converged on me at once, growling and snapping at one another. Jenny was the first to retreat to the garage roof. Hurriedly I moved the stepladder back and forth, making sure they all got equal amounts in order to avert a full-scale battle. Even with the passing of time, friendship never developed between them. Jenny remained the underdog.

"Larry, come look at Jenny's nipples," I called early one June morning as she stood on her legs reaching for a cracker.

"Yeah, it looks as if she finally has babies," he agreed.

Jenny ate the dry dog food quickly and rushed away, as if in too much of a hurry to visit with me. She clearly wanted to hurry back to something more important.

With this second year came a surge of confidence I can only attribute to maternal aggressiveness. As the city park raccoons hastened to run her off the tree-feeding station as usual, Jenny stood her ground, snapping at the other female. This complete role reversal happily was permanent, and she succeeded in keeping the park raccoons off the tree.

As Jenny kept coming regularly to the tree each evening, I rushed out to see if her babies were with her. Now that she had restored her authority over the other raccoons, she wasn't frightened at all and kept them at bay while she ate.

"Larry, Stephanie, come quick!" I shouted, nearly a month later when Jenny finally brought her babies.

Four miniature raccoons followed her closely in tight formation. Clinging tightly to the branches, they stayed close to mama. As they climbed on her back, Jenny reached around and pulled one to her. She put her arms around it and licked it all over. Clumsily climbing over each other, dangling by one foot, they inched their way along the tall branches.

"Oh, aren't they darling! Can we touch them?" Stephanie asked, enchanted.

"That's up to Jenny. We'll see when they come closer how they react to us." Jenny came to the feed box, the babies staying with her. They were not yet interested in solid food, so one or another would try to nurse while Jenny ate.

Slowly I reached my fingers up to Jenny. She took my hand and sniffed it, then continuued eating as I stroked her head. Following her attitude of trust, one baby raccoon also sniffed my hand but the other three kept their distance. I was happy that Jenny trusted us enough to share her babies. They were so much fun to watch, although it made me nervous to follow their inexperienced attempts at climbing. Even when inside the house, I generally looked out the dining-room window to watch their antics.

"Stephanie, get Papa fast. A baby just fell," I yelled, rushing outside. Surely raccoons fall all the time; it will be all right I thought to myself.

Jenny excitedly ran back and forth on the lowest tree limb, while I held the fallen female baby in my arms.

"What happened? Is it all right?" Larry asked anxiously.

"She just fell. She's dead already. Still warm," I said through my tears. She must have struck just right to have died instantly.

"I'll bury her in the orchard," Larry said, visibly moved.

Standing on the picnic table, I reached out to Jenny. It used to be "unscientific" to attribute human emotions to animals. Yet animal behaviorists, through careful field observations, have discovered a great deal about their feelings. In my obser-

Jenny teaches one of her youngsters the fine art of soliciting a handout.

vations of animals, I know they communicate with one another and me by expressing anger, fear, affection, jealousy, anxiety, and love. Because we can't understand their means of communication doesn't mean that they lack specific emotions and ways to express their attitudes.

Jenny expressed herself after the loss of her baby. She was noticeably upset and continued to pace and call to her fallen infant. After coming to my arms and sniffing my hands thoroughly, she climbed to a distant branch, put her hands under her chin, and lapsed into silence. As the three remaining babies climbed over her for attention, she ignored them and continued quietly to stare into space. She remained in that position for hours. I'm convinced she was aware that one of her babies was gone and she mourned. Whether she recognized death as an endless stillness she had seen before, or whether she knew only that one baby was gone, the effect was the same: confusion and grief.

The next day the tragedy seemed further from Jenny's mind as she and her babies put on another show for us. I worried as they continuously got into climbing predicaments. The babies appeared more curious toward me. One quickly touched my hand before scooting back up the tree. Jenny didn't mind if I touched the babies, or if Amber, the orphan fox, played under the tree, but if Heidi came out from under the trailer, she growled at the dog menacingly. Since Jenny had experienced real trauma from teasing dogs before I rescued her, I saw no point in introducing her to Heidi.

Because of her worried attitude toward the dog, I fenced Heidi off from the back yard so Jenny would feel more comfortable when visiting the tree. Heidi didn't appreciate this as she enjoyed sitting at the base of the tree, whining and watching the babies. Maybe she was reminded of a tiny raccoon orphan we had briefly years before. Heidi had cleaned it and kept constant watch over it. She was as sad as the rest of the family when it never recovered from a virus infection. But these babies were lucky enough to have their own mother. The babies screamed loudly when in trouble. Following Jenny to the garage roof, one couldn't make it over the corner extension and began crying for help. Jenny went back and clasped her hands around its shoulder, pulling it to the rooftop.

Each baby displayed a different personality. One played very shy, hanging back and refusing all crackers from my hand. One played the bold adventurer, even nibbled my fingers. The third one just observed the action while squatting in the pan of water I kept with the food. They didn't always wash their food before eating it, but because they did like to drink while eating the dry dog food, I always made sure the pan was full.

Before long, with the arrival of the hay season, we became too busy to enjoy their charades. We hadn't yet perfected our hay-cutting method and were also having difficulty with our mechanical equipment. Translated, that means the very old, poor excuse for a tractor that came with the place wasn't fit to run . . . and Larry hadn't figured out how to fix it.

I tried to forget about the hay problem as I contacted a new insurance client. She looked vaguely familiar. "Did you once live in Santa Barbara, California? Did you teach at Union Grammar School? Can you possibly be Miss Knox?" I blurted out.

"Why, Judy, are you one of my babies?" Miss Knox exclaimed.

Eighteen years is a long time to remember a fifth-grade schoolteacher. But Miss Knox was special. She still is. That is, if housing foster teenagers and operating a horse ranch for their benefit is special, she qualifies. Miss Knox's ranch is also a wildlife refuge, so meeting again as two adults we shared a common bond.

"Do you have your hay yet?" she innocently asked, after catching up on our missing years.

"No. The tractor's broken. We can't find anyone to cut and bale our fields, and we can't get any hauled this far. We may have to sell our livestock.

"Maybe my boys can help. After all, you're one of my babies," she said, her blue eyes twinkling.

Miss Knox located hay and volunteered several of "her boys." Larry and the teenagers loaded, hauled, and stacked hay for twenty-four hours. In the middle of the night, between trips, they drank soda and ate donuts while giggling over the antics of the visiting raccoons.

The next weekend we had a picnic for all of Miss Knox's Sleepy Hollow gang. Jenny won their hearts as she stole licks from twenty different ice cream cones.

One crisp night a peculiar sound startled me from sleep. Not anxious to leave the security of bed, I first considered snuggling against Larry and going back to sleep. But, as the noise became louder, its origin came to me in a flash. It was the baying of coon hounds.

While throwing my clothes on, I envisioned a terror-stricken Jenny running across the fields, leaping into the creek, scrambling toward the woods, searching for a safe place as she led the hounds away from her babies. But no safe place awaited her. She could climb a tree to escape the dogs. But she couldn't escape the houndsmen. They would shoot the raccoon. Wounded, she would fall to the ground to be gnawed and pulled apart by drooling dogs.

"Larry, wake up! Wake up!" I screamed, trembling as the cry of hounds signaled they were hot on a fresh trail.

The dogs rushed closer. We darted outside, flashlights in hand. They were on our property. Would they catch the raccoon or tree it before we could stop them?

"There's a car in our drive," Larry said when we heard the

engine. The headlights were off. How could trespassers explain this midnight intrusion?

"I'll check it out," Larry said, motioning Heidi to join him. As the two neared the car, the occupants sighted them. One man opened the car door, shouted an abusive remark, and shook his fist menacingly at Larry and Heidi.

CRASH!!

A bottle flew toward Larry, smashing against a tree, "Get em, Heidi!" Larry yelled, as splinters of glass soared past his face.

The roughneck leaped inside the car as 100 pounds of enraged dog sprang toward him. The driver stepped on the gas pedal and sped the trio away. We heard the car stop again and the men called their hounds. The chase was over. The raccoons could rest.

We returned to the trailer and worried that the men might return. We were thankful for Heidi's protection, and enraged that the hunters were not content with scouring thousands of acres of national forest available to them. They wanted our land, too.

"Hold the post steady," Larry said next weekend as we erected our gate. We cemented posts into the ground and attached a ten-foot metal gate.

"Snap the lock shut," I said, as we closed out the world.

Many raccoons have since come and gone. One little masked bandit caught in a torturing steel trap paid dearly for his only crime; stealing fish from a stocked private pond. The intervention of a visiting teenage girl saved it from death. Amid peer ridicule for such "soft" behavior, she courageously released the anguished raccoon from the trap and took it to a veterinarian. After treatment, she brought it to me for release. The bandaged paw alarmed me, so I called the veterinarian for instructions.

"I gave him shots for infections and sewed the wound with dissolving thread," the veterinarian said. "He can tear the bandage off by himself. The poor creature is so frightened it would be better to release him now."

We liberated the raccoon in a secluded part of the ranch. As a knowledgeable wild raccoon, he wouldn't need our help finding food. Thousands of U.S. Forest Service areas extending from our place assured ample room for all. Rich in natural food and waterways, it's raccoon heaven. Natural predation assures control. Bandage and all, Larry spotted the little fellow again a few days after we released him.

Nothing is so cruel as the steel trap. It should be outlawed. Millions of innocent fur-bearing animals endure agony, freezing, thirst, and hideous death because of it. In many parts of the country, there are no laws to prohibit trapping during mating and brooding season.

How many women would want to keep warm wearing fur from a fox that slowly froze to death? How many would feel beautiful wearing the skin of a mother raccoon that died tearing herself to pieces trying to reach starving young? How many would feel comfortable wearing the fur of a beaver that died struggling and gasping as water filled its lungs? It is unbelievable that women continue to wear the furs of animals that endure such intense suffering. Trapping must be stopped. Wear synthetic furs or, if you must wear the genuine article, at least buy ranch-raised furs. The animals still have to die for your vanity, but they aren't tortured besides. If there is no market for wild fur, the trapper will be out of business.

Most zoos are nothing but animal jails that should be abolished. They have outlived their indefensible excuse for existence; educating children about animals. What can an apathetic, bored, begging bear show a child about the magnificent animal he really is? Television is a much better tool to educate about wildlife. The new animal drive-through attractions seem somewhat better, at least allowing the beasts more space and company.

We wanted Stephanie to enjoy the beach before summer ended, so we took an infrequent trip down the coast. Before leaving, we noted repeated signs that proclaimed an animal attraction not to be missed. The overwhelming advertising claims made me curious to view this "Garden of Eden."

Some of the star attractions had some freedom. But the majority of the small barren pens didn't even allow liberty to run or protection from the sun. Disgusted, we were about to leave "Garden of Eden" when by chance I poked my head into an apparently empty shed. Well hidden from tourists, little shoe-button eyes looked out from a filthy cage. His paw dipping into a rusty soup can half filled with water, the large listless raccoon actually seemed to have tears in his eyes. And no wonder, in this trap-like cage confining him in his own filth, he couldn't even stretch.

"My god, Larry, look at this raccoon."

"He's probably just there temporarily."

"I'll write a letter to the Humane Society when we get home," I promised the raccoon. As the animal's intelligent face seemed to be begging for help, I changed my mind about the letter.

"Do you work here?" I asked a grubby man in dirty uniform.

"Yes. Does your gal there want to ride a llama?"

"No. That raccoon is in a terrible place. How long has he been there and when are you going to move him?" I asked, pointing toward the shed.

"He's only been there a few weeks and, anyway, it's not so bad."

"He has to have a better pan immediately, or I'm going to report this place," I said, wondering what his definition of bad could possibly be.

"Besides, I hate cleaning up after these damn animals," he said.

"What kind of idiot owns this dump anyway?"

"Why, I'm the owner," the man said.

"It's against the law to keep an animal like that, I'm warning you to move him." He didn't know it, but my harassment was still in the early stages and hadn't even progressed to the downright nastiness that embarrasses Larry into disappearing when I attack someone over an animal.

"Well, hell, if you think you can do any better, you take him," he said, spitting on the ground too near my open-toed shoes for comfort.

"You bet I will," I replied as his jaw dropped in surprise.

He shufflled off to find a cage. I wasn't too surprised that he seemed reluctant to *give* me the raccoon on his return.

"Well, you'll have to pay me fifteen dollars for this cage," he said, obviously hoping that would deter me.

I handed him the money and marched out with the caged raccoon.

"I could never make a scene like that," my quiet husband

said. "But I'm glad you did it," he continued as we shoved the cage in the luggage compartment of the station wagon.

Fifteen dollars would be missed from our tight budget, but it was a cheap price to pay for that raccoon's freedom. After arriving home, the raccoon slowly came out of the cage and calmly walked over toward us to be petted. We were amazed. This poor creature must have been someone's pet. Yet he wasn't holding past experiences against us and wanted to be friends. We named him Sammy.

Sammy couldn't seem to get his fill of water and kept returning to the large tub we placed in the yard. After living on dry corn, he was starving for good food and quickly devoured raisins, graham crackers, grapes, berries, and dry dog food. Happily running, jumping, and playfully cascading around the yard, eyes shining, a raccoon was born again.

After ecstatically climbing the raccoon feeding tree, Sammy went too far out on a limb and fell several feet. Luckily he fell onto the trailer roof and not all the way to the ground. He had probably never known freedom before and had a lot to learn about climbing trees. Hence, he wasn't anxious to try again. We paraded to the creek, anxious to introduce Sammy to more than a pan full of water. Splashing, swimming, and scampering in water over his belly, he wanted to laugh, I'm sure.

Sammy wasn't afraid of the dog and Heidi appeared eager to become friends. Lying down close to the raccoon, she would whine and stay still as Sammy sniffed her. Reaching out tentatively, he quickly nipped her paw lightly. Heidi remained motionless and seemed to pass this test.

Piercing screams woke us again in the middle of the night. Sammy tore around the base of the feeding tree, squalling in nervous excitment at another raccoon. Continuing to eat, the visiting city park raccoon didn't pay any attention. It may have been the first time Sammy had seen another raccoon and his excited screams and pacing continued from afar.

"Sammy's gone," I announced at the breakfast table. His curiosity must have made him follow the other raccoon. But he returned before we had time to worry, the other raccoon with him. Sammy seemed fascinated with this duplicate of himself. He continued to follow his new acquaintance everywhere.

Sammy struck me as more docile than any raccoon we've

taken in. He even enjoyed being held, begging for attention on his infrequent visits. From one sojourn he never returned. We'd like to think he simply outgrew his need for us.

By the time Sammy departed, Jenny's babies weren't so little anymore. They quarreled among themselves for food. However, they respected Jenny's authority and never tried to pirate her portion. As they matured, Jenny had an army to back up her menacing growls at the park raccoons, who no longer came together, so I couldn't tell them apart. Jenny's babies stayed with her through the first winter, but went their separate ways as Jenny prepared for a new family. The noisy battles in the tree continued when incompatible raccoons met, but they all got their share of food. In order to prevent dependence, we didn't supply all their food requirements, just lent a helping hand.

Soon Jenny had a new family. Her babies had babies. And if the park raccoons decided to bring their families, well . . . they did.

THREE

Education of Elijah

Stephanie and I first saw "our bear" in the children's section of a metropolitan zoo on a brisk September morning. The cub was alone in a very small cage that allowed only enough exercise area in which to rock back and forth. Weighing about forty pounds, the cub had been orphaned by a hunter.

Black bears are game animals, the season extending from August to January in Oregon. True, regulations state "no female with cubs should be taken." But not many hunters take time to determine the sex of a lone bear before pulling the trigger. Moreover, in some states the season is year round, so I suppose we should consider ourselves lucky.

Because more bears are killed each year, various state Fish and Game Commissions seem to feel that the bear population is not losing ground. They rarely take into consideration that the human population growth has produced more hunters with easier accessibility to bear country. So in reality the bear kill goes up each year, while the bear population declines.

Watching this poor dejected orphan sucking his foot, I couldn't understand why the veterinarian in charge had told us such scare stories about him. He certainly didn't seem aggressive, yet it was too hard to tell for certain with the heavy bars between us. The zoo couldn't keep him as they were already experiencing a bear population explosion. He was going to be destroyed unless we could rehabilitate him. Knowing this, we were determined to try and returned two weeks later to get him. We searched the stores for a suitable cage in which to haul the bear cub home, finding it difficult to locate one that would fit into our compact station wagon.

"That's a lot of money. Can we afford it?" Larry asked, eyeing the $45 price tag attached to a shiny metal cage.

"No. We'll just have to charge it and try to pay for it monthly. Have you got a better idea for carrying him home?"

Finally we proceeded to the zoo to pick up the bear. The attendants prodded him into our cage with pole and gloves, appearing too frightened to touch him. As we returned to the zoo office to sign release papers, I was wondering what we were letting ourselves in for. Larry looked at me and winked. I knew he was having second thoughts, too.

"Who could be honking their horn so long?" Larry asked, shouting over the blaring noise coming from the zoo parking lot.

As the vaguely familiar horn continued, our eyes met in silent communication and we bolted outside. Horn blasting, radio blaring, headlights flashing, windshield wipers frantically swishing to and fro—our car had turned into a playground for a grinning bear enjoying the commotion. (Can a bear really grin?)

"Oh brother," I said, "Lucky he didn't open the car door. Can you imagine chasing a bear through downtown Portland?"

Made for a docile dog and not forty pounds of mischievous bear, the cage had let us down. The cub was not the kind of baby to be picked up, so after thirty minutes of begging and gentle prodding by three zookeepers, Larry, and me, we finally secured him more effectively by wiring the cage shut.

"I'll drive," I volunteered, conjuring up visions of being the one to wrestle a loose bear as Larry attempted the strange freeway.

Reaching through the cage bars, the bear's claws massaged my head while he loudly moaned his worry into my ear. Combined with the radio music, which soothed him, Stephanie's ceaseless chattering, and Larry's backseat driving, my nerves were shot.

"Let's give him some warm milk," Larry suggested, hoping it would quiet him.

Spitting out the chewed nipple and swallowing the milk with one fast gulp, his cries resumed, only louder. Though jelly rolls and cream pastry were not proper fare for a bear cub, only halfway home, with the most difficult road still to drive, they seemed temporarily acceptable. It takes a lot of donuts to feed a bear, but they made the last seventy-five miles easier than

Elijah

the first. The milk and donuts soon went through him, which partly accounted for the immense feeling of relief when we finally reached the ranch.

When the bear cub was only a blur in my mind, I wanted him to be named Smokey. My first dog was Old Shep. Our bull was Ferdinand. And my horse would have been Black Beauty if she hadn't been gray. The first animal you actually own that you've dreamed about as a child has to have a magic name worthy of that dream. Larry wanted Brute or Harry. But who ever dreamed of Harry the Bear? We compromised and named him Elijah.

"What shall we do with him while we finish the pen?" I asked Larry. We had scraped together enough money to build a cage large enough to house the cub temporarily.

"The bathroom in the old house ought to be good for something," Larry answered, referring to the original dwelling on the ranch that we had decided against remodeling. We placed the open traveling cage inside the bathroom and quickly shut the door, peeking through the keyhole as Elijah started prying off the boarded windows. We couldn't worry about the bathroom now. We had work to do.

Hammering by flashlight in pouring rain for several hours, after that nerve-shattering ride, was enough to strain even the best marriage. So by this time Larry and I were barely on speaking terms. A heavy gauge, two-by-four-inch mesh wire covered the sides, top, and even the bottom to prevent him from digging out. The gravel bottom was covered with straw to protect his feet, and three-quarter-inch plywood extended around the back, top, and half of the sides to protect him from the weather. A snug, dark den box completed the cage. At six by twenty feet, it was three times larger than the zoo cage. When we stepped back to admire our hard work, we were smiling with pride—and speaking again.

Afraid of the traveling cage, Elijah wasn't anxious to be caught again. But it was past midnight and we were exhausted, unable to think of another way to carry him to the new pen. Finally we enticed him with warm milk, tricking him once again into the traveling cage and then depositing him in the new pen. Elijah ambled out, sniffed it thoroughly, and bedded down in the straw to sleep.

The next day we didn't know what to expect from Elijah. The zoo attendants had led us to believe he was wild. They handled him with heavy gloves, prodded him with poles, and jumped whenever he came near them. The bear's large teeth and two-inch claws were quite impressive, but his growl really caught our attention.

"Don't get in the cage with him," I warned Larry.

"I think it's all right. He hasn't tried to bite my fingers through the cage. Besides, we're gonna have to find out what to expect from him," he answered.

Stephanie enjoys Elijah under mother's watchful eye.

I nervously watched from outside the cage while Larry crawled through the low door. Charging full speed at Larry, Elijah jumped on his back.

"Watch out!" I called, closing my eyes.

Larry's nervous laughter reassured me and my eyes opened to see Elijah sucking Larry's ear. He clutched Larry tightly, while purring like an outboard motor. A very possessive bear, he wanted constant contact. He sobbed pitifully when Larry finally left him. We would have preferred him wild so that when released he would fear humans, but the damage had already been done by someone else. He missed his mother and obviously didn't suckle her long enough. Sucking his own foot, a habit he never broke, he continued loud slurping noises the whole time.

In possession of a healthy appetite, Elijah's food bill competed with ours. He consumed several quarts of powdered milk solution, dry dog food (my answer to everything), and buckets of apples every day. Luckily "paradise" came complete with orchards. A special treat was old bread and donuts the bakery sometimes gave us.

"How tender he is, more gentle than the raccoon," I told Larry on a warm October afternoon. I was finally brave enough to join him in the pen. While my wrist was in Elijah's mouth, I had a close look at his teeth. They were blunt and reminded me of a dog's teeth.

Elijah's education required that he have some freedom. Larry has all kinds of hidden talent, and he designed and made his own transmitter for Elijah to wear around his neck on our daily walks. We didn't want to lose him, and the deer-hunting season added to the risk. (Most bear are killed as an afterthought by deer hunters.)

It was soon apparent that Elijah didn't want to lose us either. If we ran, he ran. If we walked, he grabbed our legs, stood on two feet, and held us in a bear hug. So we ran again. Splash! With no hesitation Elijah bellyflopped into the creek to enjoy a long swim. He came out. We ran again. The daily walks were not only for exercise but to introduce him to his habitat and teach him to find food. As Larry and I dug up an anthill, Elijah finally showed some interest.

"But how many ants will fill a bear?" Larry wanted to know.

Over several weeks we introduced him to the berry bushes, apple and pear orchards, carrion, and fish. When Elijah caught his first nearly dead spawning salmon, Larry and I watched as proud parents. On these walks we were in constant communication with Stephanie inside the mobile home via our walkie-talkie units. Gentle to a bear is not gentle to a "little miss," and our aspiring veterinarian has to be satisfied to help with animals more her size.

We still housed Elijah in the cage, but his several hours of

Elijah loved to wrestle with me.

freedom each day were still better than the zoo. If only I could have convinced him of that, maybe he wouldn't have cried so loudly when we returned him to the pen. By the middle of October he weighed sixty-three pounds. We were pleased with his progress.

The horses and calves didn't know how to accept this intruder when they first met in the apple orchard. They shared their feeding ground with wild bear and knew enough to keep their distance. But could this animal clutching Larry's leg be the same thing? Ears forward and very alert, the horses charged toward us. Elijah held his ground, stood on his hind legs, waved his arms, and snorted. The horses bucked and kicked the air, and galloped off. As they returned, Elijah was the one to run, so a game of bluff ensued. The calves were smaller, but braver. They touched his nose, then ran away as a panic-stricken Elijah climbed the nearest tree. So far it was a standoff.

The daily bear walkouts fell to me when Larry, who usually ran interference with Elijah, fell down a flight of university stairs and broke his ribs. Since I weighed 115 pounds and Elijah 75, it would present quite a challenge.

It was a standoff between Elijah and the curious horses.

Contentedly sucking my arms and purring as I rubbed his head, Elijah had several minutes of quiet affection with me before our excursions began. It was a peaceful, thoroughly enjoyable time as Elijah and I investigated the surrounding forest. When he climbed high in a fir tree, I sneaked off and watched from a distance. Pretty soon he missed me and came down crying. Bear eyesight is poor, and if I stayed still he wouldn't see me. Bawling the whole time, he sniffed the air and walked around trying to find my scent.

"Here, here I am, Elijah," I called, and he happily raced to me and started sucking my arm again.

As the days passed, I had to keep well ahead of him, because his exercise period suddenly meant rougher play. Not content to hug my legs, he now tackled me from a fast run. As my legs buckled under and I fell to the ground, I couldn't help wondering how much fun it would be when he weighed 300 pounds.

After several days of being chased to the creek and back, I armed myself with a branch. Too tender to kill spiders, generally carrying them outside, released unharmed, I nevertheless hit him very lightly to discourage him from mauling me. But he rolled over, started sucking his leg, and crying at the same time. Feeling terrible, I gave in and started petting him again. Then he grabbed me hard to begin wrestling as if it were all a joke. But I wasn't laughing.

To ease my daily workouts I decided to introduce him to Heidi. I hadn't done so earlier because I thought Elijah was past the baby stage of accepting new friends of a different species. It was her biggest baby, but Heidi took the challenge eagerly, licking him from head to toe. She won him over. Now I was again able to enjoy our outings without being mauled.

Romping with Heidi provided all the exercise he needed. They tumbled to the ground in mock battle, rolling, rearing, and wrestling. Heidi pulled his ears, he chewed her neck, always in gentle fun. They took turns chasing each other, but as Heidi was faster she loped easily along so as not to discourage him. Not only fun, but good training for a bear. Hounds are used extensively to hunt bear. If he didn't fear dogs, he might have a better chance when free.

Missy, the black cat, also joined our walks. Even though she was panic-stricken by Elijah, she wasn't going to let a bear stop her from following Heidi, everywhere, including swimming in the creek. Whenever Elijah went toward the cat, Heidi jumped between them and started whining, taking the weaker animal's part, as was her way.

Rather than long walks, Elijah preferred to tumble with Heidi or sit in a treetop. When we walked in the open fields, he nervously looked around and trotted right at our heels, but if we walked near the dense forest, he excitedly ran ahead and climbed the first fir tree he came to. At the end of every walk it was reprehensible to trick him into his pen with warm milk. The only way to feel decent about it was to remember the zoo where he didn't even have that much freedom.

Larry and Elijah walked to a solitary old apple tree at the farthest end of the ranch. Elijah settled among the uppermost branches and reached for the unobtainable apples. As Larry was about to nap at the base of the tree, he came awake with a sudden start. He stood within a circle of fifteen giant bear feces, and these weren't Elijah's. In the wild, bear droppings are easily recognizable, not only by size but also by content. In the fall, apple pieces go through them without being digested. Larry was dubious as to what a wild bear's reaction might be to a cub treed by a man. An old mother bear might want to save a cub that didn't need saving. Larry had no alternative but to

Heidi and Elijah were constant companions.

wait until Elijah became anxious enough for milk to want to follow him home. But the nap was forgotten as he kept a ready eye.

Shy of people, black bears usually avoid confrontations at all costs. We were normally not afraid to encounter them in the woods. In fact, during one June mating season a large male bear had me worried for his safety. Traveling too close to the road toward civilization, he ran extreme danger. Running toward him, shouting and clapping my hands, I intercepted him and he returned to denser forest.

One of Larry's co-workers, a visiting professor, and his wife came to visit us one wet December Sunday.

"Did you remind them to wear old clothes?" I asked Larry. With so many animals to care for, we never dressed up at the ranch.

"Oh, I forgot to tell them that, but surely they won't dress up to come out here. I told them it was a ranch."

Sure enough, as they stepped out of their car, I was dismayed to see Betty Kirk wearing a fancy short skirt, high heels, and stockings. We were dressed in typical ranch attire, expecting to give them the grand tour.

"Oh, look at me, and I knew we were coming to enjoy animals. I just didn't think," Betty Kirk said. Turning down my offer of old clothes, she good-naturedly insisted that we let Elijah have his freedom anyway. We ran interference, but ninety-five pounds of Elijah still grabbed the nearest pair of legs to hug. Although he had a preference for Larry or me, Betty Kirk still went home with a lot less nylon on her legs.

Since autumn we had explored the ranch searching for the "perfect" Christmas tree.

"When can we cut it?" Stephanie kept asking impatiently.

"It's time," Larry announced one morning two weeks before Christmas.

The glistening snow lent a festive air, as we trekked through the woods with Elijah following like a second dog. He constantly whined as we sang Christmas carols. Maybe he was trying to tell us something. Whenever the bear cub wanted to grab Stephanie, Heidi intercepted with a quick tug on his fur.

"That's the tree," Larry said, pointing toward a small fir.

"Won't it die if we cut it down?" Stephanie asked.

"This one is doomed anyway because it's overcrowded. That's why we chose it."

We threw snowballs at Larry as he cut the tree. By the time we hiked all the way home, Elijah was ready to snooze in his den.

The new year meant a new beginning for Elijah. Well over 100 pounds and no longer the same dependent baby, he began to enjoy his freedom most of the day. We had an unusual amount of snow; and while his appetite tapered off, he didn't really hibernate. He spent most of the time under the old ranch house or in the tall timber of the adjoining forest. We still kept tabs on him, but not with the transmitter. If he wanted to disappear altogether, we would let him go. We didn't want to retrieve an outgrown collar.

"Hey, what's that?" said an unfamiliar voice.

"What do we have here? Len, come see what I found," said another stranger.

As we fed the horses, Larry and I heard the excited exchange in the usually quiet forest.

"Who could that be?" I asked him as we tried to locate the voices.

After stumbling through overgrown thick brush for several minutes, we came to a clearing that held four excited Forest Service surveyors. They all began talking at once.

"The damnedest thing, a bear keeps following us, tries to grab us, then runs up a tree."

"I've never seen anything like it."

"There he is, up in that tree."

"That's our bear, Elijah. We're teaching him to survive in the woods. He's tame and won't hurt you. We'll have him follow us home," Larry explained as they shook their heads in disbelief.

"We'll be working here several weeks and we'll watch out for him," the foreman promised as Elijah followed us home.

As Elijah gained strength, he played rougher. He didn't mean to hurt us; he just didn't know his own strength. Heidi could still outmaneuver him, but when he grabbed us it was extremely difficult to get away.

Suddenly Elijah bit Larry's hand, drawing blood. The bear was quick-tempered when he didn't get his way. Elijah was anxious for his warm milk and kept charging as Larry tried to pour it into the dish. He kept snapping, and it was hard for Larry to get away. I wondered how it would be when he was full grown and dominated us. But we didn't fault him. What he did was natural bear behavior. It was not his fault that our lives had intertwined.

The weeks passed and solitary Elijah was on his own. Between January and April we saw neither tracks nor the bear, though we continued to leave out dry dog food for him.

We tried to teach Elijah to accept the woods.

One night as I prepared for bed, Heidi's bark startled me. She never barked at wild animals, so when she did growl, I became concerned. Looking out the window, I saw red tail-lights slowly moving down our drive. By the moonlight I also saw three hounds running behind. The dogs were searching for a fresh trail. Were they after Elijah? Where did they come from? No one besides us had a key to our gate. Could we have mistakenly left it open?

"I'll check it out," Larry said, grabbing the gun.

I was frantic. Our bear was free. It wasn't hunting season; he should have been safe. Someone was after an easy trophy, because bear hounds were running behind the pickup.

Larry angrily returned only five minutes later.

"The gate's down! They pushed the cemented posts down and dragged the gate off its hinges," he yelled while dialing the police.

I was surprised how quickly the police came. We met Trooper Stevens of the Oregon State Police Game Division.

"I was patrolling the area because it has a high rate of poaching and night-hunting," Trooper Stevens explained. "Now tell me what happened."

The following week Trooper Stevens conducted a thorough investigation. Because of tire tread and paint color left on the gate, he thought he knew the guilty party. However, there was not enough evidence. He could only issue a warning. We found our gate wide open a few mornings later while leaving for work.

"They've cut the chain this time. But at least they left the gate. Trooper Stevens' warning must have helped some," Larry said as we viewed our broken lock and ripped apart NO HUNTING and NO TRESPASSING signs. "I don't want to leave the animals here all day without a locked gate. I'll stay home and have Trooper Stevens come out again," Larry said.

By reporting the incident, we wanted to assure the trespassers that we would prosecute. There was the danger that whoever pushed down our gate might discover the ranch was left unwatched for long periods. What might happen to our wildlings required little imagination.

"I'm really glad you guys moved here. This area is filled with poachers and, because so many are related, it's been impossible for me to catch them alone. With your help, I can do it," Trooper Stevens told Larry.

"Here. Take a key for our new lock. Come whenever you want," Larry said.

"I'll stop by here at odd times while you're at work and make sure all the neighbors are aware that we watch *this* place closely," Trooper Stevens volunteered.

That gave us some relief as we labored all day in the city. But time went by, and we still hadn't seen Elijah.

Larry and I were deep in the world of high finance, playing

Elijah was always ready for a ride.

Monopoly, when the phone interrupted our wheeling and dealing.

"My name's Ben Cannon. I live on the coast and travel one of the back Forest Service roads to work at the mill. Can I bring my family to meet your bear?"

"We haven't seen him in months. We don't have him any more."

"Why, I see him begging for handouts along the road every morning on my way to work," Ben said.

"What else do you know about the bear?" I asked unbelievingly.

"One morning he was nearly killed by Skinny. I saw Skinny's hounds had him treed and I told Skinny to call off his dogs because it was a tame bear. When the bear came down and licked him, Skinny said it almost made him want to give up bear hunting."

"Go on. What else?"

"Another time one of the forest rangers saw him begging for food and, knowing he was tame, put him in his back seat and drove him back to your place. If you don't mind, we're gonna go look for him," he said as he hung up.

We were astounded at these revelations of Elijah's close

whereabouts. It was hard to believe, but in three months he had *never* come near the trailer nor answered our frequent calls.

"Let's go look for Elijah, too." I voiced what we both wanted to do.

"Well, first we have to find the calves before dark," Larry said.

It took over an hour to locate the calves. By that time, Elijah had gotten in trouble. Ben Cannon and his family found Elijah. He was docile while they fed him honey and stroked his coarse fur. But when the honey ran out, Elijah didn't understand and scratched the daughter while searching for more. Luckily it was only minor, but how minor would it be when he reached maturity?

The bear had been able to make it by himself the first couple of months. But during this last month strangers had made a park-begging monster of him. It was with mixed emotions that we found him lying on his stomach across the narrow road, chin on his arms, begging for handouts. Happy to see us again, he certainly recognized Larry and me, but he no longer seemed fond of Heidi. He no longer growled and bit her in fun. Heidi retreated to the car. Maybe the bear hounds caused him to dislike all dogs. Sucking Larry's hand, Elijah willingly followed him through the tall timber toward home.

"I'll stay with Elijah," Larry said, as he invited the bear into the old ranch house with him. Sitting on the sofa together, they renewed their friendship. Elijah clung to Larry and bawled as he did when a baby. Sitting there for hours comforting Elijah, Larry worried about the bear's future. Elijah had been his favorite, and now there seemed no good way to handle the enigma.

We were willing to pay or to transport him any distance ourselves. This was before drive-through parks were so plentiful, so I called Crater Lake National Park and others. The answer was always the same: "We don't want another half-tame bear; we have trouble enough with the ones we have." The zoos had enough bears; the parks had enough bears; only the forest had room for him. But because he had lost his natural fear of humans there was a risk involved for him.

However, the Game Commission had to make the final decision, as he was still under their jurisdiction. In view of Elijah's

The bear cub was Larry's favorite.

recent escapades and close calls, they recommended we transport him to a wilderness area and described the location to me. We bribed 150 pounds of bear into the rear of the station wagon and headed for the designated area. We were a quiet crew, except for the low sad vocalizing of Elijah as he sucked his paw.

"Does this look like a good area to you?" Larry asked.

"It's far enough from everything, but there's so much logged-off stuff. Let's keep looking," I replied.

After several hours of driving the back gravel logging roads, we thought we had found an acceptable location.

"Let's hike him away from the road as far as we can," Larry suggested.

We trekked a couple of mountain ridges away with Elijah at our heels. The timber here was tall and dense, just the way Elijah preferred it. Quickly we dumped sacks of apples and donuts to occupy Elijah while we sneaked away. Looking back at his forlorn face, I felt like a mother abandoning a child. Sneaking a glance at Larry, I noticed his green eyes were watery.

I wish we had never heard of Elijah again. That way we could have clung to hopes of his survival. He could have made it, but man interfered again. Too many logging roads intertwined everywhere. Man has penetrated all of the forest.

Elijah wandered back to the dead-end logging road. That would have been fine, because after losing our scent he would still have been in a dense forest area. But late one evening an old logger who had drunk one too many was anxious to have people believe that he had shared beer with a bear. He coaxed Elijah into the rear of his pickup and drove him all the way out of the wilderness area to a small town. In town the people put him on display, chained in front of the city hall. Several of the intelligent, good-hearted folk wanted to take him back to the woods and release him. Emotions ran high on both sides of the issue.

An Oregon State Police game officer whom we didn't know, entrusted with wildlife welfare, made the final decision. He shot our Elijah between the eyes. He was too anxious to shoot first and ask questions later. He gave the age-old excuse for killing wildlife: "Rabies." A ridiculous statement that went unchallenged.

We learned of this tragic ending only after Elijah was already dead and it was too late to help. If we had it to do over again, we would have gone to any length to put him in an inaccessible area, perhaps helicoptering him in. Maybe that's wishful thinking. Our funds were limited and we had no one to help us.

Elijah had a good life with us and enjoyed some freedom. That's more than his original destiny was to have been. But those thoughts do little to ease a pain that will never go away.

An affectionate cub, Elijah frequently requested a bear hug.

FOUR

Who Gives a Hoot?

The year after we lost Elijah stands out as the year of the owls. Screech, barn, and several great horned owls came to us within a two-month period. Never before nor since have we had so many owls at one time.

When I hung up the phone I wasn't too excited. The young voice indicated another sea gull nestling was coming to dinner. After several in one week, I had just about reached my sea gull limit. I should have been suspicious when he told of finding this "large-beaked, big-footed bird at the base of a fir tree in the downtown Eugene cemetery."

After a hard two-hour drive, a long-haired, bearded, sensitive-looking young man stepped out of his VW camper. Wrapped in an electric blanket was a tiny ball of white fluff so new to this world its eyes were still tightly shut.

"I didn't know what to feed it," the young man explained. The bird's only diet had been lettuce and water during the two days he had been captive. The nestling was so weak by the time we received it that chances for its survival seemed slim. As warmth was essential, I made a tiny nest of Kleenex inside a wooden birdhouse and placed it on a heating pad. Then the birdhouse was placed inside the clothes hamper and moved beside my bed.

From its claws and the position of its eyes, we determined it was a raptor (bird of prey). Hunted birds have eyes on the sides of their heads to allow them all-around vision. Birds of prey have forward eyes so the visual field enters both eyes. It was too early to make a more positive identification, although we suspected some kind of owl. We named him Spook in honor of the cemetery.

An eager eater, Spook made up for lost time. His chittering every two hours sounded like music to my ears. I didn't mind

As a fluffy nestling, it was difficult to recognize Spook as a screech owl.

not getting much sleep; the important thing was his willingness to live. I started Spook on canned cat food, tiny pieces of chicken liver and hearts dipped in egg yolk. As soon as food touched his whiskers, his mouth would fly open to expose a bottomless cavern. Because all owls and hawks swallow their food in one gulp, they need roughage to assist digestion. The indigestible part is then rolled into a pellet in the stomach and regurgitated almost daily. To supply this roughage for such a tiny baby, Larry had the great idea of drying eggshells in the oven, then crushing them and spreading the pieces on bites of food. This diet seemed to agree with the noisy ball of fluff. He thrived.

In a mistaken effort to hurry his strength, I fed Spook ground chuck. This proved too rich, causing diarrhea. Spook's little bottom lost feathers, became red and sore. I applied mineral oil after washing it with warm water. In a day he returned to normal. Hourly offerings of baked egg custard with vitamin drops restored strength lost by the diarrhea. After the second day of this routine I put him on a four-hour schedule.

Spook's eyes opened on the second day we had him, so we judged him to be approximately two weeks old. As I was the first creature he saw, his instinctive "imprinting process" must have marked me as his mother. Larry had a chicken that called him "mother," so that, besides reading about imprinting, the phenomenon was a living experience for us. Larry found abandoned the last egg of our mother hen when it was nearly ready to hatch. He heard a stir inside and kept it warm. While cupping the egg in his hands, a little chick popped out. From that day forward, that rooster refused to follow the regular chicken routine. We showed him his real mother and placed him under her breast. But after living on a heating pad the first few days of his life, Jasper refused to believe heat came from above and always nested on the hen's back. When the frustrated mother finally kicked him out, he returned to the house to live as a pet, following Larry everywhere.

One of Spook's toothpick-like legs jutted out at an odd angle, so that he held it tightly to his chest and limped when he ventured his first steps. As the veterinarian examined him, the uncooperative patient, Spook, chirped madly and snapped his beak.

"I don't think an X-ray would find a break at his young age," Dr. Lyon said. "But why don't you call Dr. Sims for his opinion? He has a pet owl and is more knowledgeable than I."

"Bring your prize right over," Dr. Sims invited.

As doctors and laboratory technicians at the University Veterinarian Diagnostic Laboratory hovered over him, Spook kept his cool, just bobbing his head about and watching intently. The prognosis was that his malformed and swollen leg would straighten out by itself as he grew. They thought it had been injured by the high fall out of the nest.

"The coloring is the same as my great horned owl, but, at three and one-half ounces, this nestling is much smaller than mine was." Dr. Sims was explaining why he correctly pegged him a screech owl.

When taken out of his nest box for a frequent visit, Spook snuggled under my chin and softly cooed to me. He loved attention, closing his eyes in ecstasy as my finger rubbed his head.

"Whooo whoo whoooo." Over and over, Larry was making noises like a screech owl when suddenly Spook gave him a disdainful look with those huge yellow eyes and uttered his own perfect call, a tremulous whistle or trill—not bad for a two-week-old baby.

Spook grew rapidly.

Spook's baby fluff disappeared fast, replaced by different shades of gray feathers. He was also more alert. When I imitated his clucking noise, he watched me intently and answered. When I was out of reach he flapped his wings and hopped as closely as possible to me, climbing up my leg to nest on my lap.

For such a small bird, his wing span seemed large—about twenty inches. He flew three feet from the bed to my lap before his fourth week. A few days later he flew across the living room. Now no longer caged, he enjoyed the freedom of our home. He was not much trouble. I merely threw a handkerchief over his favorite perches—chair back, lampshade, refrigerator. He sat for hours looking like the proverbial wise old owl, but was not much larger than a parakeet. One of his favorite pastimes was perching on the bird cage and teasing Sunny, our yellow parakeet.

Spook also had the freedom of my office back room. He was a good traveler, and I didn't want to leave him alone for long periods when he was a nestling. As he matured, he was content to sit for hours near the warmth of a light bulb and wait for the attention I bestowed on him between servicing my insurance accounts.

Although owls are normally nocturnal, they can see just as well in daylight. Spook adjusted his schedule to ours and slept quietly in our bedroom the whole night. He was personality plus, with definite likes and dislikes at an early age. Expressing his feelings by regulating his ear tufts up or down, he conveyed several expressions. Although known as ear tufts, they were decorations only and had nothing to do with hearing. His ears were located on the sides of his head. When Spook was happy and calm, he was short and plump-looking, with his ear tufts hidden in his feathers. When he was angry or frightened, he stood tall and slender, ear tufts standing straight up.

Visitors from town were always an occasion for us, and good friends like Kathy and Mick Martin were really special. Spook generally took people at face value and liked what he saw. However, with ear tufts standing on end, beak clacking and head bobbing, Spook stretched out his full five inches and glared at Mick. Instant hate was unusual for my friendly owl.

"It must be your beard and long hair. You just don't look like the rest of us," we teased Mick.

After the Martins returned to town, I temporarily housed Spook in a large cage, which was not to his liking. He grabbed the bars and chittered until free again. "Owl, I have no intention of making you a prisoner." I explained why the cage was a necessity for his own safety when company came, while traveling in the car, or when the cats were inside.

Neither cat nor dog scared him. Standing tall, raising his ear tufts, and flapping his wings at the black cat, he scared *her* from the room. She hid behind the sofa.

"Don't be fooled, Spook, Missy eats birds."

Without waiting for a formal introduction, Spook flew to Heidi's shoulder and pulled out a mouthful of hair. But Heidi, accustomed to such goings-on, merely looked at him and went back to sleep.

During Spook's first summer with us, a business trip to Portland became necessary: six days of insurance schooling for me, while Larry and Stephanie enjoyed ice skating, swimming, and the comforts of a plush motel. It didn't seem fair, but after Larry bought me a lovely new coat, it became bearable. I didn't like to leave Spook, as I was sure no one would dote on him as I did.

"Are you sure they'll let us have Spook in our motel room?" Larry asked as we approached the attractive motel where the insurance company had reserved our rooms.

"Well, I called and asked if they allowed birds. The clerk didn't ask what kind. That's all I know."

We covered Spook's cage and walked boldly by the reservation clerk, who assumed we had a parakeet. Smiling at him, we didn't say "yes" or "no," just continued straight ahead to the elevator.

"Ah, the ice machine's handy," Larry said as we hurried past it to our room. I knew my husband wasn't thinking of bourbon on the rocks, but Spook's liver chunks that had to be kept cold. Spook enjoyed the freedom of the large motel bathroom for seven whole days. The easy-to-clean porcelain and tile made a perfect cage. He even had his first bath in the tub. Splashing, dipping his head under water, he loved it. Chittering angrily, he discovered he couldn't fly with wet wings and had to be content to join the towels on the rack. Before the daily maid service we returned him to his traveling cage and covered him. At night, when I returned from classes, I held him close to give him the daily dose of affection and handling that he loved.

Continuing to hand feed him, I had inadvertently encouraged his reliance on me. While I attended classes all day, Larry planned a surprise. Leaving the liver and chicken hearts on a dish in front of Spook, Larry refused to believe he couldn't feed himself. Ignoring his squawks for bites, Larry only changed the food as it dried out. I would have given in. Hours later, clutching a liver piece in his claw, Spook brought it to his mouth and took a bite. At long last Spook could feed himself. What a time saver that was!

Spook was as happy as we were to return to familiar surroundings. City noises are nice for a change, but they can't compare to wind whistling through the trees, the creek splashing against its bank, or coyotes howling in the distance.

Spook accepted all additional wildlings without alarm. Then suddenly we acquired a great horned owl that shared the summer with us. At five ounces Spook was a perfect miniature of the three-and-a-half pound great horned owl. What a fine dinner little Spook would have made for the large raptor. Larger owls prey on smaller birds, although ninety percent of their diet is made up of rodents. One quick look at the great horned owl and Spook was more frightened than he'd ever been. Clinging to my shoulder, he dug his sharp claws into my skin as his large eyes watched this giant intruder. Spook couldn't know that the thoughts of the great horned owl were only on his own recuperation.

That same summer, Heidi and I had an exciting encounter with a wild coyote. As we trekked through the pasture, hoping for a glimpse of the elk herd, a coyote loped into view. It saw us and bounded away. As we continued our hike, its fear of me gave way to an intense curiosity about Heidi. It trailed us, playing hide and seek. Heidi's sable color and shepherd traits do resemble "God's Dog," so the coyote's inquisitive nature was understandable.

"Go ahead," I encouraged Heidi to meet her canine relative. Calmly she approached the coyote, which stood still. They encircled each other, the coyote lowering its tail and Heidi holding hers aloft, signifying her dominance. They touched noses. The coyote forgot my presence as they danced an acquaintance. After a few rare moments, Heidi bounded back to me and the coyote ran away. On subsequent walks, Heidi and I were frequently aware of that coyote escorting us.

Spook spent the warm summer days in a large outdoor cage. The sunshine felt good to his little leg, which never grew normally. The cage was large enough for flight, but Spook saved his flying for the evenings spent in the living room. Although he could sometimes catch moths and insects to supplement his diet, his flying never progressed to the long flights that would be necessary if he were free. In his fall from the nest he had also sustained a wing injury that never healed properly. Thus there was no question of setting him free, although my heart ached when he answered the wild screech owl calling to him from the orchard near his cage.

Knowing only his life with us, Spook was quite happy in his limited freedom, except during mating season . . . when he fell in love with a dirty sock. Flying with it, hopping, pulling it behind, carrying it everywhere, he wouldn't let me replace it with a clean one. Clacking his beak, flapping his wings angrily, raising ear tufts on end, Spook was angry with me for the first and only time in his life. That sock was his security blanket or mate, I'm not sure which, but it made him happy.

The pellet he regurgitated told of an interesting life he had hidden from me. Pieces of thread, yarn, carpet, and dog hair told a story of the grounded wanderings of a tired little bird. As Spook grew older, he spent more and more time at his favorite perch, Stephanie's top bunkbed, beside the window. Eyesight keen, he could spot a hawk when I saw only an unidentifiable speck. Angry and scared epithets spewed from his mouth, as he pulled himself up to his full six inches.

Spook was not at the window one day. It was a day just like any other when we returned from work. Calling and listening for his wooo whooo answer, I became frightened at what I might find. In a dark corner under the bed I found Spook, stilled by death. His over-all health was never vigorous. He finally weakened and hopped to a cover of darkness to sleep forever. We enjoyed him for nearly two years, and even now the call of a wild screech owl in the orchard brings tears to my eyes.

Have you ever seen a bird caught in a pole trap? The bird lands on an object that looks like a utility pole. Steel jaws slam shut on one or both legs. Steel tightens on broken flesh as it yanks the bird upside down to twist in the wind, hanging by tortured legs. The raw leg wounds turn gangrenous and begin to rot . . . the bird is still alive, eyes glaze over in agony until released by slow death or the trapper's bullet.

Mr. Madison raised gamecocks. Around the perimeter of his farm he had several pole traps. After two hawks and one owl endured slow death, Mrs. Madison called me. The CLOSED sign went on my office door. As we drove the 100 miles to the farm, Larry warned me to hold my tongue for the sake of other birds we might save later.

"You must be crazy to come all this way for only an owl," said the red-faced, pompous man who owned the gamecocks.

"Yes, but I wouldn't go across the street to save you." I mumbled it quietly to appease Larry, but it did nothing to vent my frustration.

As the traps were not checked every day, the owl had been hanging by his legs a full day. Before we arrived, Mrs. Madison had cut him down, then tied his raw, broken legs together, and threw him in a burlap sack to wait for us. The owl was obviously in shock and didn't try to move when we untied his legs and laid him in a box of rags.

"He looks dead," Larry said when we arrived home.

"After two hours of that rough drive, it wouldn't surprise me."

But the owl's large yellow eyes focused an ominous stare upon us, and his ear tufts were raised ever so slightly. His raw swollen legs still stuck together with the dried blood. As an adult great horned owl, he stood nearly two feet long, with a wingspread of four feet and a powerful beak that could have done real damage to our bare hands. But as Larry bathed his legs in warm water, gently forcing them apart, the massive bird quietly endured our treatment without a struggle. Could he have known we were trying to help?

The owl needed more treatment than we could offer. I decided to try a different veterinarian. The one we had been patronizing for years never had any enthusiasm for our wildlife work, always charged what the traffic would bear, and even thought we were a little crazy.

"CHRIST!" exclaimed Dr. Sampson, the new veterinarian, visibly moved by the torn, mangled legs. I liked him already. He explained he would take X-rays, administer an anesthetic, pin the leg, bandage it, and give me medication to take home—all for a minimum sum because of the wildlife work we were doing. The X-rays showed one leg had two tendons severed, and both legs were badly infected. Dr. Sampson pinned and put a splint on one leg, treated, sewed, and bandaged the other. He gave us full instructions on caring for the wounds. When I picked Owl up, he was still groggy from the medication, but he had been a good patient.

"Don't tell anyone I undercharged you, because I won't do the same for someone's pet hawk. I don't believe in caging wild birds, but what you're doing is different," he said.

"I won't, but you're getting yourself in trouble, because I

always have something like this that needs help," I replied, thinking he'd back out.

"You bring it in and I'll keep helping you," Dr. Sampson answered.

Fantastic! I had met a veterinarian with compassion.

Owl wouldn't accept food. Most hurt birds won't. It became necessary to force feed him. Larry held Owl on his lap and opened his beak while I stuffed warm chicken hearts and liver pieces down his throat. These were coated in Cosa Terramycin, a bird medicine, and must have tasted terrible, but he swallowed. The splint had to stay on several weeks, and we had to change the dressing on the leg daily. We were happy to do it, but this added significantly to our time-consuming duties. Our wildlife work kept expanding, but time and money kept shrinking.

Owl came to work with me as he also needed the Cosa Terramycin three times daily. My back room sometimes became busier than the front office.

At home Owl had the freedom of the bathroom. Twenty-two inches long, with a wingspread of more than four feet, the small room was an affront to this proud, mighty raptor.

Every evening as Larry and I struggled to treat his wounds, the pain in Owl's eyes was agonizing to me. As the medication was applied, Owl's head rested against me, ear tufts down, eyes closed, mouth shut. He never tried to bite. He trusted us. Owl enjoyed attention. As I scratched his head, he nestled against me and closed his eyes in contentment. A week passed and we no longer had to force feed him. When I offered food, he carefully took it from my hand, never mistaking my finger for dinner. We added small bones and roughage to his diet so he could regurgitate the pellet necessary for his digestive system.

We took another trip to the Madison farm. A second great horned owl endured the torturous trap. This one was probably the mate to the first. A pair of owls mate for life and occupy the same territory. They keep their range clear of other great horned owls, although they will allow in other raptors. Larger than the owl we already had, this one was probably the female.

The female owl didn't have the severe breaks her mate had. We applied ointment to the open wounds and fed her medicine for several days. When it appeared the injury would not hamper her chances for survival, we released her at our secluded ranch.

"Will you never heal?" I spoke through tears to the male owl as he watched his mate fly to her destiny . . . alone.

After two months of intensive treatment, it was time to remove the splint. Excitedly I watched as Dr. Sampson began cutting it away. Again Owl was a courageous patient. He had such a will to live.

"It came off with the splint . . . the leg came off with the splint," I managed to gasp before starting to cry.

"Let's put him to sleep," Dr. Sampson answered. "I'm afraid his legs were just too far gone."

As Dr. Sampson carried the noble owl away, he clacked his beak and fought to stay with me.

I am thankful to have known Owl. During his valiant fight for life, he showed intelligence, courage, and taught me respect and love for his kind. Thankfully, there is now a federal law against steel-pole trapping of owls, hawks, or any birds. This is strongly enforced by the Federal Bureau of Sports Fisheries and Wildlife. Predation claims or wild bird abuse should be reported to that agency. Trained wildlife personnel will trap the individual raptor in a humane trap that permits live release in a remote area.

The beautiful barn owl Dan Elliot brought to us was very different in appearance from the great horned owl. The snowy white heart-shaped discs on his face and the beautiful brown and white plumage on his body made him a handsome bird. He was also lacking the ear tufts common to great horned and screech owls. His claws were thinner and needle-point sharp in comparison with the great horned owl's blunter, stronger-looking talons. As the sharp points dug into my arm, it was hard to remember not to get excited or tighten up. An act like that would make him clench his hooks tighter.

This barn owl had been raised as a family pet, even traveling on long car trips with the young couple who had stolen him from his nest. As he grew, it was apparent that apartment life was really too cramped for his welfare. Having a change of heart, Dan decided to give him his freedom at our place.

Clinger, the barn owl, had been used to hand feeding from

birth, so Dan got a batch of tiny mice from the university and started training him to catch his own food before bringing him to us. Our plan was to wean him from human interference, and to that end we purposely did not attempt to continue the close relationship Clinger had with the Elliots. It was hard to resist his overtures of friendship when he cooed softly, his head completely upside down.

Clinger's hunting tactics had to improve before he graduated to freedom; yet a cage would be too confining for that.

"Again, the old ranch house would be the perfect solution," Larry suggested.

An adequate number of rodents were already living there, and the large empty rooms would give the owl plenty of space to fly in. We added tree stumps and branches to make him feel more comfortable, but trees scared the apartment-oriented bird. However, he slowly gained confidence and flew to a branch to taste a leaf. He also found a bug while climbing the tree trunk, and his soft eerie whistle bespoke his contentment. Larry also nailed roosting perches in several locations, but his pellets and droppings showed a strong attachment to the sleeping box he grew up in.

"This ought to bring the rats out," Larry said, placing grain on the floor in several areas. We would also supplement his diet with chicken necks, hearts, livers, and giblets until Clinger could feed himself. He ate by grasping food in his foot and feeding it into his mouth.

The barn owl's completely noiseless flight is one of the reasons his hearing enables him to catch rodents in complete darkness. The sound of wings would interfere with this ability. Located under the facial discs, the ears of owls are larger than those of any other group of birds.

We consistently checked Clinger's pellets for indications he might have been catching his own food. Other than that, we left him alone, except for changing his water and leaving the supplementary chicken pieces. Dissecting the small dark hairy pellets, we were excited to find indications he was capable of feeding himself. After allowing him a few more weeks of practice, we opened the attic window, but let him choose his own time to leave. Initially taking nightly forays into the outside world, he left for good one autumn night. We were delighted

Clinger the barn owl was tame when he came to us.

to free him on our land, where he could help control the rodent population.

Over the years we have continued successfully to release other owls in this same manner. By the way, that's one house Larry got to clean.

FIVE

Vivacious Vixen

The ranch rodent population never stood a chance. The emancipated owls threatened from above . . . foxes were the ground patrol.

Hobo had been an unhappy city fox, confined in chicken-wire caging. Alone for long periods as an adult, he was no longer tame, even toward his owners. He had been stolen from his den as a baby by people who claimed to love wildlife. With a late change of heart, they had realized how unhappy he was and had asked us to set him free.

"Be careful. He even bites me," his foster mother said, using heavy gloves to put him in my traveling cage. This was hard for me to understand. Any fox I've had since a baby could always be handled without biting. Some people make the mistake of trying to force or punish a wild animal instead of letting the animal decide upon acceptance. Also, my foxes were always part of the family, not just caged rarities.

Foxes are hard for me to resist. Since it was winter when Hobo first came, and our mobile home was empty, I let him come inside before turning him loose. Weary and watchful, but not really frightened, he kept his distance. To show how crazy I am about foxes, I moved my sleeping bag into the bathroom with Hobo and slept there for two nights while he walked all over me. I had hoped my quiet presence would alleviate his fear. However, he couldn't be won over, and I accepted his hostility as natural and even preferable for his release. If I didn't have this "thing" about foxes, I wouldn't have tried. I'm convinced that once past the baby stage, foxes rarely accept strangers.

Coughing and trembling, Hobo also refused Heidi's friendly overtures. He had enjoyed dog friendships before, but, unlike raccoons, he wouldn't accept another. Twisting and struggling,

Hobo was a twelve-pound armload of trouble. I barely managed to carry him to the bear run. After feeding him there for several days, we opened the cage door.

"Where'd he go?" Larry asked, camera in hand. Hobo disappointed us by disappearing into the overgrowth immediately.

The fox vixen tenderly licked her young before leaving them to hunt for food. She would never see her babies again. As she stalked a mouse two men stalked her kits.

"I'm gonna place the dynamite right here at the burrow entrance. When that fox comes back to nurse her young, I'll blow them all up," the farmer told his companion, who later relayed the sad tale to us.

"Now wait a minute. You didn't tell me that's what you wanted the dynamite for. I'm not gonna let you do that," his companion stated. As a graduate student in zoology, Tim was aware of the important role played by foxes in the "balance of nature." He also realized any knowledgeable farmer would be pleased to have a rodent-consuming fox family protecting the grain supply. "If I take the babies, will you let the mother live?" Tim asked, unable to convince the farmer of their worth.

"I suppose so. She won't hang around with her babies gone anyway."

Tim unhappily took the babies. Only one survived the early separation from their mother. Recognizing the limits of his city apartment, the student sought a suitable home for the kit. After searching several places and learning that the Game Commission destroys all foxes, coyotes, and other non-game animals brought to them, Tim offered the baby to me.

"Now you're sure you can take care of Amber properly?" Tim asked anxiously for the third time.

"I'll do my best. We've had foxes before, and I'll give her plenty of love and attention. She won't be lonely."

"All right, but I'll check on her often," he promised, feeling uneasy about leaving her with a complete stranger. I couldn't blame him.

A grayish imp nearly three weeks old, Amber explored my office. Behind the sofa, under the desk, inside the counter, no place was overlooked. Curiosity overcame her fear after she accepted me. Because she was still so young, she hadn't developed the fear of strangers that would soon come. I have found that once a fox's eyes change from blue to yellow, at approximately eight weeks of age, they rarely fully accept people. Amber slept snuggled in my arms during the entire drive home.

Once again, Heidi had a new baby and she was thrilled with Amber. Amber buried her head in my lap. She was frightened as this large animal came toward her. Stealing a glance as I sent Heidi away, her eyes fixed upon the dog's long bushy tail. Amber's whole attitude changed immediately. Leaping out of my arms, she ran after Heidi, excitedly whimpering. Did that tail remind her of her mother?

Heidi licked her all over, enduring Amber's sharp teeth biting her ears and tail. Trying to nurse from Heidi, Amber couldn't understand why "mother" was always empty. Her claws dug into Heidi's stomach as she sucked.

Often likened to a cross between a dog and a cat, the fox kit is much more alert, inquisitive, and intelligent than a kitten or puppy of the same age. Amber constantly explored.

"Where's Amber going to sleep?" Larry asked, as if he didn't know the answer already.

"With us, of course. Don't you want her to?"

"I don't care." My good-natured husband laughed as he grabbed and hugged me.

Amber started out on top of the covers near our feet, but as the night got colder she inched her way up until she snuggled under my chin. At her age she still slept for long periods. She woke me only a couple of times during the night. Watching her walk over Larry's sleeping form, I was thankful he was a sound sleeper. His mustache twitched as her tiny cold nose sniffed his face. Laughing quietly to myself, I covered his head with the sheet as Amber bravely jumped off the bed to explore. Too little to climb back up alone, she scratched the headboard until I lifted her to my chin.

Amber recognized a kindred soul in Stephanie . . love at first sight between girl and fox.

"Amber, come get the sock," Stephanie called every evening as they spent hours noisily chasing each other the length of the trailer. I kept still. Our only child needed a good friend.

"Amber, come back with my sock," Larry called as the fox

took another treasure to her secret hiding place under the bed. Rarely tearing apart anything, Amber instead covered socks, slippers, toys, everything with her own potent scent. Come to think of it, what better way to teach Larry and Stephanie to put their things away!

This communication scent gland is two or three inches from the tail base, near the top of the tail. It is very strong when first released and offensive to most people, but I found it invigorating and could even recognize fox odor while walking in the woods.

Amber was too young to join Heidi outside all day and would have been too lonely by herself. Since I couldn't leave her a solitary prisoner at home, Amber went to work with me. She soon became a good traveler, riding back and forth in the cat-carrying cage several times a week. My back room made a perfect dark den for her long naps. A kitty-litter box helped solve the mess problems. However, there was only a fifty-fifty chance of her hitting the cat box, so Pine Sol became a strong odor in the back room.

At home, litter boxes accented the décor in every room. When she awakened I promptly deposited her in one and she used it. I think I was the only trained one. Finally as the days went by she used it more and more. One thing Amber could not curb was her natural excitement every time Heidi, Stephanie, or I appeared after a few hours' absence. Whimpering, ears back, tail down, panting, running excitedly, she exuded musk. This was natural. I accepted it and used more Pine Sol. I never scold a wild animal. As for Amber, she was a fox entitled to her unique fox ways. There were enough domesticated animals in the world. I was not about to turn her excited greetings of love into fear by spanking her as she greeted us in the only way she knew how. I did, however, cover the living-room sofa and chair with blankets and the tables with newspapers. The use of her tiny claws made sharp scratches, there being no difference to a fox between coffee table and floor.

While Amber was small, the cats would have been a real threat to her, so we penned them up. An acquaintance I once knew had a sad experience mixing kit with cat. The aggressive cat's claw took the eye of the baby fox in one fast swipe, upon which the people shot the fox to end its misery. When Amber was mature, she and the cats respected one another naturally.

Amber as an impish kit.

Anyway, springtime arrived and baby birds left their nests. Enough casualties befell the young as they learned to fly without my well-fed cats eating them. So, even if there had been no Amber, the cats would have been temporarily jailed. Every year barn swallows by the scores returned to nest on our porch, in our barns and garage. We welcomed these insect eaters with open arms. Amber couldn't catch anything that spring, and the barn swallows accepted her below the nest as they did the dog. But let a cat happen by and these brave parents turned into miniature kamikaze pilots as they dive bombed their enemy.

After watching several foxes over the years, I am convinced that adult foxes capture fewer birds than domestic cats. As quick as a cat, they are not as sly and the birds have time to fly away. But foxes are far better rodent catchers than cats, prancing along, enjoying the hunt as they do life. They are able to pounce accurately onto a field mouse six feet away.

"Shh, what's that noise?" Larry, the usually sound sleeper, was wide awake, nudging me. "She's ripping the box springs apart. You've got to put her out, Amber's gone too far this time."

No longer content to be under the bed, Amber wanted to be in it. Larry had already lost several books, shoes, socks, and slippers because of her; and his slow fuse was ready to ignite. Usually I don't give in that quickly, but, as it was the middle of the night, my foggy brain couldn't think of a ready solution. So I agreed.

"How about nailing chicken wire across the frame bottom?" Larry suggested the next morning.

"Great idea. When can you do it?"

"Not me. She's your fox. You can handle it. Besides I have to dig fencepost holes, work on the tractor, and change the oil in the car." He had me there. I only had to clean house and do the laundry.

As I hammered the chicken wire in place, Amber seemed very upset at the change. Whining and crawling in and out of the box spring, she was only partially pacified by the hammock-like blanket I nailed to the bottom for a den.

Stephanie was Amber's companion in mischief, and I smothered the fox with affection. This paid off in complete acceptance and a remarkable social attitude toward the two of us.

"Help me! Ouch!" cried Stephanie as Papa pretended to clobber her. This play-acting is for Heidi's benefit. Stephanie enjoyed having Heidi rush to the rescue, knocking Larry away. Heidi would rescue Stephanie, me, or the cat; but if Stephanie or I pretend to hit Larry, she ignored his call for help. Unexpectedly, this time Amber was upset, too. Too timid to be forceful, coughing her excited bark and running around, she grabbed Larry's pant leg and tried to defend Stephanie.

"Lets see, is it six candles for the birthday girl?" I asked, pretending not to remember.

"No, Mama, I'm seven," my daughter corrected me as we both saw a flash of orange near the ballerina birthday cake. "Oh no." Amber had joined the birthday celebration without waiting for an invitation. Laughter filled the kitchen as we watched her dance off the table with frosting falling from her mouth.

Meeting her first fawn initially, Amber scampered across the sleeping deer not at all frightened. As for the deer, wasn't Amber just another cat?

As Amber grew older, she was no longer content to sleep quietly in the back room at work. I decided to leave her home sometimes. Locked in our bedroom, which she considered her den area, she made out fine. Prancing with ears back, tail down, excited musk gland, she welcomed me after work. Then all over again for Stephanie and Heidi. Next time I resolved to be smarter, to have all converge at once, then only one release of musk.

Summer evenings after work were spent picking a few sprigs of apple blossoms, as Amber, Heidi, goat, deer, and I walked through the orchard to one of the beaver ponds. I was struck by the absolute stillness of our peaceful valley. Our beaver neighbors made many ponds by damming the creek in several places until it overflowed. They lived in lodges built of mud and sticks. One main lodge usually had two entrances, a central chamber above the water level, and a ventilating chimney connecting the chamber with the top of the lodge. Finding the main lodge, I quietly put my ear to the hole on top. Squeaking little sounds signaled that baby beavers were already in residence in the central chamber. How pleased Larry was when I told him! He wanted to resume his daybreak observation time at the creek. Sneaking away from our warm bed, he sat for hours in the rain waiting to glimpse a beaver or an otter. I preferred to sleep in and do my watching at sunset.

Formerly trapped for their pelts, the beaver colony made quite a comeback when we moved here. At dusk in the summer evenings or in winter's pouring rain we spent hours sitting quietly by their lodges watching for them. What a thrill when they no longer felt it necessary to slap a warning tail against the water!

Beaver ponds and dams hold back large quantities of water during flood season and equalize the flow during summer, so that surrounding pastures are wetlands of a dry summer. The horses and cattle enjoy lush grazing during the dryest months. Another benefit are the many alder trees they cut. After eating the twigs and smaller branches, the beaver leave neatly trimmed trunks. Quick to discover work-saving ideas, Larry collected the poles and used them for fencing.

As my animal companions and I walked back past the barn enjoying the cool beauty of the spring evening, Amber disappeared under the barn floor. Returning with a dead mole in her mouth, she was ecstatic but unwilling to share it with us. Afraid we would confiscate such a prize, she buried it, digging with her front paws and covering it with her nose. Not well hidden. She uncovered the rodent and found a new spot.

"Amber!" I called, tired of any game that shut me out. "I want to go home." Amber was too young to be left on her own, and I was worse than the clucking hen when it came to supervising my babies. While waiting for Amber, I took in the lingering sunset. Our valley vibrated with unseen activity. That we could actually protect scores of animals made the days in my office cubicle bearable. Finally satisfied that she had hidden the mole in the best place, Amber was ready to head home.

"The water's out again," Larry announced from the shower stall. Grumbling to himself, he slammed the back door on his way out to check the filter. "Damn it!" I heard him curse. In the dark yard he had tripped over another fox hole and didn't appreciate the added inconvenience. Already grumpy from a difficult day at work, a hard drive home, a cattle feeding by flashlight (a windstorm had taken the electricity from the barn), he now had to scramble up the side of the mountain to release the spring.

Amber had a passion for digging huge holes, but rarely filled them up again. Some of her holes protruded under the fence.

Heidi enjoyed Amber's constant attention.

She dug deep for dens, not escape routes. Her digging seemed to slow down after she made a deep dark den under the laundry shed. Preferring to stay warm and dry, she usually denned up during heavy rains.

We added another fawn to our growing summer family.

"Watch out for Amber!" I yelled a warning to the fawn. Little baby-teeth nips from our constant bundle of energy sent the deer leaping into the air. Amber was too small to harm the deer, but I separated them anyway.

Our wildlife family kept growing. Another raccoon joined us.

"Amber, watch out for Cookie!" She had met her match in the mature ex-pet raccoon given to us by a humane society. Tugging at Cookie's tail, Amber learned a short lesson: not everything runs when teased. Snapping and growling, the usually good-natured raccoon turned on Amber. It was lesson enough to discourage a playful fox.

Finally that summer, thanks to my father, the laundry-room shed got a new floor. My folks lived in the same city where we worked. They took care of Stephanie much of the time, and sometimes helped out with ranch projects. Over seventy years old, my father was still agile enough to roller skate with his only grandchild, and although my mother's health wasn't good, she gave our trailer a good spring cleaning once a year. While Dad did the jobs Larry didn't do, and my mother cleaned my oven, Sheppy, their thirty-five pound dog, became acquainted with Amber. Cautious yet wanting to be friendly to the stranger, Amber ran up, only to meet Shep's curled lip. Old age made him grumpy. A smart dog, he showed his teeth only if he thought no one was looking. Grabbing Shep's skinny tail, Amber teased him constantly, not threatened by the dog's growl.

Leaving Shep temporarily, Amber watched Heidi drink from the water bucket. That was always an invitation to play. Amber crouched on her stomach with front paws extended, head on her paws. Then as Heidi trotted away from the bucket, Amber jumped on her head, sat on her back for a moment, then tumbled off to the other side.

As Amber grew older, she no longer tried to be friendly with visiting dogs and uttered her frightened, coughing bark and dashed to safety. Only Heidi remained her friend, and I was thankful for this when I released her.

"Marie and Paul will be spending the night Friday," I reminded Larry. "Will you make your delicious pancakes?"

My handsome husband is an excellent cook. He bakes the Thanksgiving turkey, pizza, and bread from scratch, shish-kebob or any time-consuming gourmet treat that takes the patience I lack.

Although our visitors, the Gregorys, are senior citizens, they are newlyweds. To be a part of their optimistic enjoyment of life is a treat that chases away my worries about aging. We gave them our bedroom and shared a bunkbed in Stephanie's room. Amber and Heidi moved in with us.

"Tell me another story, Papa," Stephanie teased. Giggling together, the three of us are the same age for one night.

After Saturday-morning breakfast, deer, goat, dog and Amber tag along for an enjoyable walk. How extraordinary that the only visitors to walk the entire length of our ranch are a seventy-six-year old man and his bride.

"Take me. Take me," Amber seemed to say, jumping at my legs. Try as she might, Amber just couldn't walk that distance and scrambled to nap under a cedar log.

"Amber, Amber." Ignoring my frantic calls, the contrary fox made me dig her out. I carried her the rest of the way.

Weeks of Amber-interrupted sleep had made me grumpy. That evening, after our visitors left, when Amber started tugging at my hair, nibbling at my toes, ready to make a night of it, I put her in the fenced yard. She scratched at the front door and, when that didn't work, moved to the bedroom window. Too much. My nightgown flowing beneath my parka, I gathered her up and carried her to the bear run a quarter of a mile away. I had never been so brave before, alone in the woods at 12:30 A.M. But now Amber could play all night and I could sleep. What a feeling of relief!

"You mean *you* couldn't take it?" Larry skeptically asked the next morning.

Waking up refreshed though guilty, even I couldn't believe I had forsaken my spoiled darling. I rushed to retrieve her before leaving for work.

"She's gone! Amber's escaped!" I sobbed, running back to the trailer in the rain. The cage that had held bear, dog, cat, and bird had let me down.

"She couldn't have gone far," Larry said calmly, continuing to shave.

"I'm not going in today. I'm going to stay and look for her."

"I'm a few minutes early. Let's go together. Maybe we can tell what happened," Larry suggested.

The claw marks around the cage showed that an animal on the *outside* had frantically tried to engineer an escape. This other animal helped Amber by spreading the heavy mesh apart, forming a squeezeable-sized hole, we concluded after carefully investigating all tracks. There was no doubt about what happened. Solitary Hobo, the lucious red and gold male fox we had released from this pen earlier in the year, was attracted by Amber's excited lonesome barks and had come to claim her. Seen infrequently, Hobo was known to be a constant visitor at the same time we had Amber. Now these footprints around the cage told a story of moonlight dancing together. We thought Amber was too young for midnight escapades.

"I can't stay here any longer while you search for Amber, I'm going to town without you." Larry said.

"Amber!" Stephanie and I searched the entire brushy area surrounding the cage. The drizzle had turned to rain, but I welcomed it to hide my tears as we frantically kept looking. It was a glum day spent in useless pursuit.

Now that I had uninterrupted sleep, my worried mind wouldn't be still. While Amber was still a baby, a great horned owl could carry her off, or a hunting dog could easily catch her. These thoughts were plaguing me as I heard a noise at the front door. Scratch! Scratch! Was I dreaming?

I rushed to open it, and Amber dashed in. A miniature tornado swept over the recently uncovered velvet sofa as Amber, yipping excitedly, wet her greeting. Twenty-four hours in the woods! Now she was ready for the warm bedroom again. Spewing up a tiny mole in her excitement, she was starving for cat food. Her happy playfulness knew no bounds as she started a new assault on my sleep. Larry resigned himself to Stephanie's upper bunkbed for that night. On succeeding nights Heidi baby-sat with Amber in the yard. No longer lonely, the fox allowed me to sleep.

Clever enough to know the exact time I arose each morning, Amber scratched at my window five minutes before the alarm sounded. This "scratch" actually sounded more like tearing the side off the trailer. Leaping four feet in the air, all six pounds of trouble hit the siding with a thud—over and over, until I went out to greet her. It was not breakfast she was after, just "good morning!"

Amber loved to be petted and used this same method to call me outside for early evening attention. If I ignored her leap against the front door, she pounced against whichever window I was behind. As she looked to me for affection, she approached Stephanie for play. Immediately when she saw Stephanie, Amber rushed for a pink slipper, hoping a game of chase would ensue. She was very obvious in her choice of playmate. If she was in a mood for Stephanie's play rather than my petting, the slipper would be in her mouth. She would never give up until Stephanie went out to run with her. She didn't have to talk to communicate.

Too tiny to boss Heidi, Amber recognized the dog as the dominant canine, greeting her with tail lowered and absolute stillness. Heidi kept her tail raised to indicate pecking order. This is not to say that Amber never got her own way. A delicious bone in Heidi's mouth called forth all her wiles. Wishing she had the goody, Amber pounced on Heidi's head and grabbed the bone while Heidi growled her off. Feigning hurt feelings, Amber then rolled on her back, crying pitifully and waving all four feet in the air. When Heidi continued to ignore her, Amber grabbed the toy slipper, tossed it in the air, and danced around as if to pretend she'd forgotten the bone. When that ploy failed, she ran to me, pulling on my pant leg until I bent down to take her. Finally driven to jealousy, Heidi left the bone to come push her head between us. Amber rushed to the bone and bathed it with her musk, so Heidi would never want it again. Then Amber proudly pranced off with her prize.

Our three spayed female cats had distinct personalities and completely different ways of treating Amber. Older and often grumpy, the beautiful green-eyed black cat, Missy, was afraid of Amber and often hid. Although twice as large as Amber— she was completely unnerved by the wily fox.

Tootsie, the yellow cat, wandered up one day as an abandoned kitten and had remained a fixture ever since. Thinking her position precarious, however, she was the best behaved of the three. Tootsie, who was afraid of nothing except Missy, ignored Amber and allowed the fox to play catch with her tail or share her food.

Cupcake, Stephanie's small Siamese, was afraid of all dogs except Heidi, all people but us, and all strange animals except Amber, whom she chased. Cupcake had no front claws and was smaller than the fox, so she really could do Amber no harm, but her threat was enough to make the bluffing fox leave her alone.

Prancing, not walking, hopping, not jumping in order to catch a bug from thin air was play, not work, for Amber. The cocky little imp was always the supreme example of enjoying life to the fullest. Waging a continuous war on the flowers, Amber kept all blossoms snipped from my red rosebush.

I watched Amber while tending the grass. Why mowing the lawn should have been one of *my* chores was never satisfactorily clarified to me. But so long as Larry continued to serve me Sunday breakfast in bed, I continued to mow with alacrity.

One jump in the air, a fall, a whimper. Amber was on her back.

"Oh my God, she's dying right in front of me!"

Not even bothering to shut off the mower, I noticed Amber still moving and yelping and feared some internal pain. She refused my touch, still whimpering. Testing her balance, she tried to stand. As she put her front paw down, it came up with a jerk and she hobbled away on three legs to the farthest and narrowest space beneath the trailer. After pleading and cornering her, I finally received permission to pick her up.

"Larry! Come quick! Something's happened to Amber."

Larry's presence disturbed her because she had never fully accepted him, but this time it was impossible for me to examine her foot and hold her squirming body at the same time. Larry reached for her paw and jerked back quickly when she tried to nip him. She was equally mad at me, but never attempted to bite me. Holding her mouth gently on my finger she pleaded with me, but didn't bite.

Having finally scrutinized the paw by the bathroom light, Larry discovered the problem.

"A bee stinger!" he said. He removed the onerous pique with tweezers. Outside again, she was her nimble-footed self. Quite a performance! Everything she did was a production.

Hearing strange noises right beneath my feet, I thought we were experiencing mouse problems. With three cats and a fox in the yard, who but Mighty Mouse would be brave enough? The last thing I wanted to do was crawl on my stomach through the cold wet night, but Larry didn't volunteer.

"You better check on your animals," he said.

Their owner fluctuated with the time of year and their behavior. My flashlight located a gaping hole between the bedroom floor and the outside insulation. Two bright eyes belonging to a wiggly, furry body shone out from a connecting tunnel. Eyes and body jumped out at me. I lay pinned to the ground. Fearful of a giant wood rat, I covered my head with my arms. When the creature started jumping up and down, I knew it had to be Amber, the practical joker. With only the usual mumbling after the hammer had hit his thumb instead of the nail, Larry boarded up the underside of the trailer. We outsmarted her again . . . temporarily.

As Amber matured, she preferred the out-of-doors. The same confusion and noises she grew up with now seemed to make her nervous. Still invited in, her visits were quick and disastrous. If I blinked my eyes, she took a bite out of the sofa, pooped on a chair, or grabbed dinner off the table. Unless I could watch her every minute, I preferred to visit her outside or in the laundry room. Shedding her buff-colored baby fluff, she grew a thick and luxurious coat.

Foxes can't climb trees, right? Then how did Amber get to the ten-foot-high raccoon feeding station in the back yard fir tree? Curious about the goings-on in this busy tree, she now busily devoured the raccoon graham crackers. Jenny Raccoon shared only with her babies and quickly threatened Amber with mayhem. It was a standoff until I joined Jenny's side.

Succumbing to the temptation to badger Jenny again, Amber climbed so that I could see her do it. Not climbing in a feline sense, she took off with a running start that gave added impetus to carry her up the trunk. The annoyance compounded the problem of keeping crows away from the "coon-bread."

"Leave it to me," Larry said.

After thinking about it for two weeks, he hammered a sheet of thin aluminum around the tree base. This solved the problem . . . again, temporarily. But then we had a new vexation. The shrill, angry screams of raccoon interrupted our television viewing. Always squabbling over their handout, the raccoons sometimes shoved one another off the feeding platform. Bolting outside, we found a frightened raccoon unable to climb over the metal that Larry had wrapped around the tree trunk. Amber stood ready to attack. An adult raccoon could easily take one small fox, but nobody had told the raccoon that. The raccoon retreated under the trailer, with Amber in hot pursuit.

"They'll work it out," Larry said, going back to the TV.

Every few feet the raccoon made a short snarling stand, then quickly took off again. Snarling, growling, shrieking came from the raccoon. Amber was ominously quiet as she grabbed bite after bite of fur. Independent Amber paid me no heed. The coon was wild. So all I could do was try to herd them toward a fence opening. Turning her back on Amber, the raccoon enlarged a hole under the fence and escaped. I blocked the hole against Amber's exit, as the coon, shaken but unhurt, scampered down the mountainside.

One night we stayed in town overnight when the wind raged with hurricane intensity. The still disastrous conditions the next day made it imperative that we check the animals. A massive mudslide had closed the main highway home. We left Stephanie in town with her grandparents and forged through a twenty-mile gravel Forest Service road. Anxiously trying to get home before dark, we sped around trees, over mudslides, and through the overflowing river. I didn't know which to fear more; the storm or Larry's driving.

"Watch out! The road's caving in!" I yelled to him as we narrowly missed the river bank at one precipitous spot. Three barns leveled, branches and debris littering the road, fallen power lines—the mute message of 100-mile-an-hour winds.

The first fir tree across our private driveway worried us. The second one scared hell out of us. Pushing and pulling, we rolled them down the bank as the heavy downpour drenched our coats.

"Do you think Amber and Heidi are all right?" I screamed.

"What about the horses and calves? Look at the river! They could be trapped!"

Our own private mudslide made it impossible to drive from the gate to the trailer. We ran the rest of the way through the storm on foot.

"It's still here! The trailer's still here!"

"I can't believe it!!"

"But the barn's gone!"

One leveled barn and five uprooted apple trees later, we acknowledged the blessing that the animals had weathered the storm. As I tossed the horses some hay, Amber and the fawns heard my call. They greeted me ecstatically. Large heavy cages had catapulted through the air, landing several pastures away. Thank heavens they were empty at the time! We wondered where we would house new orphans next spring. We couldn't afford to rebuild the cages, never mind the barn. The second barn, now minus doors and boards, was still in usable shape. Most of our land was high ground, and only the lower pastures stood under water.

The mudslide complicated our busy schedule. We had to shovel, drain, and ditch the knee-high ooze from the driveway. For several weeks, until it was driveable, we backpacked in pouring rain eighty-pound sacks of grain, fifty-pound sacks of dog food, groceries—everything—the quarter mile to the trailer. If this unusually rainy and icy winter had been our first on the ranch, it might have frightened us off. As it was, we had come through many winters unscathed and actually found them exhilarating.

Even though Amber was free, early every evening she wiggled through a small hole in Heidi's fenced yard and scratched at the door until I joined her. Now that she was catching her own food, she wasn't crazy about special bones I saved for her visits. She came home for the complete enjoyment she derived from having her neck stroked while laying on her back, eyes closed and paws lifted in the air. Jumping at me until I reached down to her level, she communicated without vocalizing. Except for an occasional light grasp of my wrist, she remained still as I petted her. If Heidi came to interfere, Amber coughed snappishly, exhibiting marked jealously. Heidi let her get away with it. After our affectionate visit, foxy Amber chased and chewed on benevolent Heidi, then danced back to the woods. Amber had the best of both worlds.

Each day Amber survived improved her chances of a long life. How well she knew her territory was a matter of life and death. Normally the life span of a wild fox is short, because of man's interference. Each year thousands of foxes are shot, trapped, or poisoned, whereas a caged fox might live as long as a dog. Still, if Amber could have seen the pathetically unhappy, lonely, bored fox I saw in the small, sterile, artificially lighted indoor cage at the Portland Zoo, I know which life she would have chosen.

Let me repeat again that foxes don't make suitable pets! However "cute" Amber might have been, she was a wild animal and required unusual treatment. Because of the shy introverted nature of foxes, they need very special handling. A caged adult fox is nervous and unhappy. A released fox needs a much larger territory than most people have to offer. Unless released on very secluded acreage, a half-tame fox won't last long because of human interference.

Moreover, when it is fashionable to have raccoon or fox pets, it means death to thousands more. Unscrupulous pet traders usually kill the mother animal in order to capture the babies, which they pander for profit. Although many pet shops give the impression that all the animals they sell come from bona fide animal farms, that isn't true. Whenever an offer is made to

Though surviving in the wild, Amber visited daily for a dose of love.

sell surplus orphans, the buyer is usually doing more harm than good. I don't believe in purchasing these babies because it keeps the supplier in business. Anyone truly interested in wildlife welfare would *give* an orphan to a good home, where chances of survival, freedom, and a normal life in the wild might be realized.

SIX

Fawn on My Pillow

Suddenly it was summer—after all that rain. A warm July evening. Stephanie was finally in bed, Larry and I exhausted. Pulling weeds . . . repairing fences . . . trimming horse hooves . . . chasing our herd back from the neighbors' pasture for the third time in one week. The last was a downright embarrassment, because we hadn't been able to afford a bull. The heifers were turned on by the imposing Black Angus stud, Tony, next door. They had already forgotten the times we sat up with the sick, found the lost in the woods, and fed the hungry all winter. They were ready to chuck it all and run away at Tony's first sexy bellow.

Reluctantly I dragged over to the screaming phone.

"Would you be interested in an injured fawn?" Trooper Stevens asked.

We suddenly came to life. Dragging Stephanie from bed, we hit the road for the fifty-mile trip to the trooper's house. In his living room we strained our ears to overhear one side of the ensuing telephone dialogue between the trooper and his superior at the Game Commission.

As game animals, deer are under the strictly supervised jurisdiction of each state Game Commission unit. This is as it should be, because too many people interfere anyway by removing perfectly healthy fawns they find in the woods. Human interference is directly responsible for many deaths each year. The law prohibits keeping native deer as pets.

Some of the Game Commission biologists were not in agreement with our treatment of injured fawns, but because of bad public relations they didn't like to admit that their solution for wounded animals was a "hit over the head." With enough healthy orphans to care for, they begrudge the extra time and money spent on animals that they view only as living targets for hunters. In our belief that a short, secure life was better than no life, we intended to keep caring for them.

New to the Oregon State Police Game Enforcement Department, Trooper Stevens didn't agree with their often callous attitude and had already made up his own mind that this fawn would be given a chance. He finally convinced his superior officer. The Game Commission had utilized us before, having long been aware of our many years' involvement with wildlife. Once convinced to let the fawn live, they agreed we would be the obvious caretakers.

It was 11:00 P.M. when we first saw our fawn. Brandy was lying in a flower bed, shaking with fright. He had been rescued from a mauling by loose dogs.

"The dogs chased his mother away. Then they surrounded him. The fawn was sinking in mud, feet held fast, as the growling dogs ripped the fur right off his back. He was in shock when we arrived," Trooper Stevens explained.

Innocent-looking, tail-wagging pets turn into savage killers when they find an animal to chase. I knew of a dachshund that killed sheep. Dogs are responsible for killing deer without even touching them. After being chased, even a mature deer can die from becoming windblown. Rural dogs should not be allowed to run free unwatched.

The shrill bleating, "Baa! baaa! baaa!" that Brandy let out as Steve and Larry threw a blanket over him took days for the trooper's neighborhood to forget.

"How will you carry him home?"

"He'll just have to sit on my lap all the way," Larry answered. Completely wrapped in a blanket, after the initial struggle, Brandy had no choice but to behave well.

When we unwrapped him in the living room, the fawn looked like an early Christmas present. Fifteen pounds of delicate spotted beauty, but marred by a torn ear and gashes on his back and face. We swabbed and treated the wounds with Nitrofurazone antibacterial powder. I concocted a solution of powdered milk, pabulum, Karo syrup, and warm water, but he wasn't having any. I used a regular baby bottle, enlarging the nipple to allow easy passage of pabulum. As Brandy continued to refuse the bottle, I held his mouth open and squirted in a few drops at a time.

"This reminds me of trying to teach those baby calves to drink from a bottle," I said to Larry.

Finally Brandy understood the warm milk was coming from the smiling clown bottle. He began sucking on his own. His little tail wagged quickly back and forth like a baby calf or lamb sucking from its mother.

"Larry, you know where he'll sleep, don't you?"

"I don't care, honey," Larry answered as we scooted the tiny fawn toward our bedroom. All through the night I checked him frequently and offered formula. He needed every sip to regain his strength.

Brandy changed overnight from the wild, frightened captive to a docile member of the family. The quiet close companionship of sharing the stillness of sleep settled his fears.

Would he be afraid of Heidi? I expected so because of his recent mauling by dogs, and, therefore, introduced them in the living room, holding Heidi still and allowing Brandy to make the first move.

"Here comes the baby, Heidi, be tender with the baby. Give the baby a kiss." These were the same words of introduction I always used to acquaint Heidi with a new member of the family. Heidi trembled in her excitement but didn't move. Brandy walked up unafraid and Heidi began licking him all over, even stimulating the bowels and cleaning it up, behaving as she did with her own pups long ago. An astonishing friendship began as Brandy quickly became her favorite.

Brandy followed as we trooped down the stairs outside, and into the yard. Over this large fenced domain surrounding the mobile home Heidi reigned as queen. The gentlest of dogs, Heidi never harmed or chased another animal, but I don't believe any dog should have the unwatched freedom of the forest.

Lilac, magnolia, hydrangea, sweet peas, and rose petals . . . all ended up in Brandy's stomach. Small satisfaction that deer fertilizer causes the grass to be greener.

While Stephanie spent hours babbling to Brandy, Larry and I repaired the pen we hoped to keep him in until he matured. The pen had a decent shed and plenty of natural browse. Approximately seventy by 140 feet, it made the perfect area for him to grow in.

Stephanie meets a perfectly formed Velvet Prince.

"Do you think we'll ever finish?" I asked.

Perspiration ran off our bodies after hours of working in the hot sun. I gave up first and retired to the bedroom for an afternoon nap. Larry and Stephanie swam in the icy creek. Running, jumping, and hopping are tiring to a small fawn, so Brandy decided to nap also. He didn't see me and thought he was alone in the bedroom. Bleating like a lamb, he was up and bawling at the bedroom door.

"Brandy, here I am."

After sniffing me, he settled down for a two-hour nap. The pattern was thus set, and togetherness became our way. Naturally housebroken, preferring to do his business outside, the fawn was easier to care for than a puppy.

Brandy was lost . . . and Trooper Stevens was speeding to reach us with another disabled fawn. After depositing Brandy inside our prize pen, we had finally torn ourselves away from him long enough to grab supper. When we rushed back out to comfort the fawn, we discovered the pen empty.

"He couldn't have jumped over it! How did he escape? What'll we tell Trooper Stevens?"

"You cover the orchard, I'll take the beaver area," I directed Larry.

Suddenly we were startled by a solitary figure strolling up the driveway. "Hi, I'm Josh Miller, your new neighbor from 'bout six miles down the road."

"Nice to meet you," we greeted him. And at any other time we would have been delighted to make his acquaintance. Josh was a retired Los Angeles policeman highly spoken of by Trooper Stevens, and we welcomed him to the community as an immediate ally. But right now we had problems. Brandy was missing. It was growing dark. Trooper Stevens was due. We couldn't explain the situation to Josh because one of the stipulations from the Game Commission was that our wildlife enterprise remain confidential.

I grew frantic as Larry and Josh engaged in a longwinded discussion about inventions, totally ignoring my ill-mannered hints suggesting that Josh come back another time.

"I can't possibly find Brandy before dark," I thought sadly. What would the fawn do when he became hungry, cold, or frightened? Many misgivings plagued me.

"Find Brandy. Find Brandy," I whispered to Heidi. The dog sped off. Did she have Brandy's scent? I couldn't even be sure she knew what I expected of her, but it was our only chance. I pursued Heidi through the orchard, across the pasture, toward the beaver pond. "Find Brandy," I shouted as darkness enveloped us.

Heidi stopped and began whimpering. She raced back and forth, trying to communicate with me. She had found Brandy, serenely nestled in the thick undergrowth. I could not have found him alone. With a quick lick of her tongue, Heidi implored the fawn to follow us toward home. I was so proud of my intelligent dog. Heidi, Brandy, and I hid in the orchard until Josh bid adieu, ambling out just as Trooper Stevens arrived with the other fawn.

"Where do you want her?" he asked, knowing us well enough to carry the deathly ill female inside.

"In the bedroom, of course." His eyes expressed his amusement.

The fawn had been picked up by tourists after they had seen her lying in the same place two days in a row. They kept her in their garage twenty-four hours, then took her to a veterinarian, who prescribed warm water with salt for dehydration and advised them that possession of a fawn was illegal. They then called the police, who delivered her to us in off-duty hours.

"We really don't expect her to live, but I know if anyone can pull her through, you two can," Trooper Stevens said as he left.

It did appear that she was too far gone to live. She was dehydrated, her gums and tongue were gray, and she was too weak to stand. She kept her jaws tightly clenched, and there was a continuous gurgling in her stomach. I gently pried her jaws open and squirted in a few drops of bitch's milk, Karo, and salt. Larry gave her an injection of two cubic centimeters of penicillin and vitamins. Cat-napping only, we took turns watching her all night long and offering nourishment. She didn't live, but her last hours were made as comfortable as possible.

For the first time Brandy was ousted from the bedroom to the shed, as his healthy playfulness would have been further torture for the dying fawn. Brandy spent the first few hours in the throes of a tantrum, striking the walls with his front hooves. Permitted back in the bedroom the next night, he returned to his favorite spot. No doubt about it, he was spoiled. But what fun spoiling him!

A few days later the shed and pen were empty and waiting, but had to wait awhile longer because neither of us could kick Brandy out of the bedroom. It had become his room, too. Screech owl, deer, dog, and us. Was it any wonder that we slept with the windows open?

Thud! Four tiny hooves landed on my stomach signaling the 2:00 A.M. feeding. This became regular routine, Brandy never uttering a sound or jumping on Larry by mistake. After drinking the contents of the bottle, he followed me outside and quickly relieved himself. While waiting, I watched the wild deer in the orchard and reached up to pet visiting Jenny Raccoon. An enjoyable quiet interlude. Returning to bed, I snuggled up to Larry's warm body while Brandy snuggled up to Heidi. We all quickly fell asleep again.

Only once did the usually quiet Brandy disturb our sleep

unintentionally. The walls vibrated as Brandy frantically attacked them with his front hooves.

"Protect the mirror," I yelled, grabbing Brandy as his foot shattered a favorite statue. "It's all right Brandy," I comforted him. He quickly regained his composure.

Had he suffered a nightmare about the attacking dogs of his youth?

Brandy took four to six ounces of my powdered milk and pabulum formula four times daily—morning, evening, bedtime, and 2:00 A.M. After reading a pamphlet stating the nutritional value of various substitutes for mother's milk, I switched his formula to the bitch's milk it more closely resembled, but this disagreed with him. When I switched back to my old formula, he thrived. I also added moist leaves and peeled apple bits to his diet. As Brandy grew, the scars on his back were covered by hair and only his tattered ear reminded us of his close brush with death.

The usually cautious cats didn't hesitate before rubbing against his skinny legs. Brandy looked down, cocked his head, sniffed them, and began licking the Siamese, Cupcake, on her face. Cupcake loved it, and we were enchanted watching her turn her little face this way and that to appreciate this new attention. Cupcake grabbed Brandy by the face and nibbled gently. As Brandy started to walk away, she grabbed his leg with her front paws as if to hold him. Whenever Brandy napped outside, one of the cats was sure to be curled up next to his tummy.

"Larry, watch Heidi. She's trying to teach Brandy to play with her." Heidi carefully jumped at the fawn. Whirling and running a few steps away, she continued this until Brandy started to chase her. How funny to see a fawn chasing a German shepherd! Heidi slowed down when the fawn dropped too far behind. Now Brandy wanted to play his way by striking his front hooves at Heidi. Brandy never actually hit her, and they began to take turns chasing each other. This game of tag continued in the orchard until, panting from exhaustion, they both fell down to rest. Following Stephanie, Brandy charmed her by hopping when she hopped. Dancing and throwing his legs in the air, he seemed to mimic her as they cascaded around the yard. If left alone, he bleated like a lamb. As he was a very sociable animal, we wanted him to have a companion to share his lonely hours while we were working.

"A young goat," Larry suggested. So that's how a cream-colored toggle billy goat named Moab, complete with moustache and horns, came to be standing on the car seat butting, biting, and kicking me all the way home.

Approximately the same size, goat and deer eyed each other and squared off. After a short scuffle to determine the dominant one, Moab assumed leadership and friendship began. They shared alfalfa and rolled barley corn, but Moab was greedy, intent on stoking in more than his share as quickly as possible—the exact opposite of Brandy. The cattle and horses were just as selfish, although I've found in every instance deer will eat unhurriedly, preferring to share. I stood guard to make sure Brandy got his fair portion.

Moab bugled, bawled, and howled. For all of his sassy bossiness he couldn't stand to have Brandy out of sight. The goat was a good choice as he and Brandy really seemed to like each other. Between nuzzlings they butted, reared, and chased each other.

Daisy, Larry's lively 75-year-old mother, visited us from Arkansas. A kind-hearted woman, she appreciated my animal insanity and always helped me on her trips to the ranch. Brandy was still the perfect gentleman and allowed inside, while his friend Moab was not. Hearing a commotion in the bedroom, Stephanie, Daisy, and I hastened to check. Jumping, kicking his heels, twisting his body, Brandy was bouncing on our bed, having the time of his life. Until his tongue hung out from exhaustion, he bounced up and down. We three laughed until our tears ran down our faces. Brandy had invented his own trampoline and had taught a new game to Stephanie.

Before horseback riding could become a favorite summer activity for Larry, Stephanie and me, we had to locate an experienced pony. Trigger, a well-mannered silver stallion with flowing mane and tail, seemed the perfect solution. Stephanie fell in love with him at first glance. We kept him separated from the mares as Stephanie acquired confidence in her riding ability.

However, riding together was our goal, so Trigger had to meet the ladies. Besides Gay and Duprey's Firebrand, there was Happy, an unmanageable pony; Coco, a gentle old mare; and Spice, a miniature pony.

At the first meeting, Trigger became a sex maniac. Having led a monk's existence for several years, he flipped out. Trigger was a beauty to behold as he reared, pawed, and snorted. The ordinarily friendly mares struck each other, kicking and biting in a jealous rage.

"I'm not gonna ride him again!" Stephanie exclaimed. All her riding confidence disappeared as she watched the battle.

Frustration stalked Trigger in his never-ending attempt to breed. More than twice his size, the mares were unreachable in more ways than one. Trigger was dangerous. As Larry and I rode our horses, the stallion chased, reared, and pawed the necks of our mounts. Finally we had Trigger castrated, but he still didn't settle down as the weeks flew by.

Brandy got along fine with the mares, which is to say they ignored each other. But chasing Brandy was another one of Trigger's vices. That cinched it. Our expensive mistake had to go. We forfeited selling him in favor of giving him to a good home. We enjoyed a quiet life again, and so did he.

Out of money and a riding pony, I turned to Spice. She had never been ridden and I didn't have much faith in my ability as trainer nor Stephanie's as novice rider. Spice has always been a pampered pet because of her unusually tiny size. But Spice's trust in us is evident. From the moment Stephanie jumped on her back, she's been the perfect pony.

With the whole family able to ride together, Heidi and Brandy tagged along. Deer who have an adequate supply of food generally stay within a relatively small area. Thus it was an easy and natural way to introduce Brandy to his yarding territory.

Goat, deer, dog, and cats also took frequent walks with us. Brandy would hop into the underbrush and disappear for minutes at a time. His exploring finished, or if he became frightened, he called a drawn-out "baaa" and frantically caught up with us. Brandy was still too small to be on his own, but the walks and rides we took were good exercise.

After the incident of the vandalized gate, police warnings and Trooper Stevens' unpredictable patrolling had kept trespassers off our property. Our fence and gate remained untouched. Our NO HUNTING and NO TRESPASSING signs stayed posted. But hounds, unable to read, traveled through fences. Hounds could easily kill Brandy or bother our pregnant cows. Don't believe it if a houndsman tells you his hound is trained only to chase bear, coon, or bobcat (as if that is acceptable). Hounds are often left alone all night on a trail that has turned cold and will bother anything. I've seen them circle our cows. One attacked me after biting Spice on the nose.

One night the baying of hounds drifted through our open bedroom window. Immediately recognizing the sound, I awakened Larry.

"Hounds are here!"

"For God's sake, not again," he grumbled, searching for the light.

Hunting is supposed to stop at dusk. We called the Game Police, as they had instructed us to do. It was 2:00 A.M., but Trooper Stevens quickly responded.

"I'm gonna check all cars on the logging roads around here. Why don't you see if you can round up the dogs?" he suggested.

"Here, boy. Here, boy," Larry and I called, after locking up Brandy in the shed. What to do with the dogs once we captured them was another matter. The first time hounds had been harassing our livestock I had decided to "play it nice" and return them to their owner.

"Keep your dogs off our land," I warned. "We keep our own dog locked up, so we don't want someone elses' bothering the wildlife. Besides, they pester our young calves."

"I can't help where the trail leads," the owner answered, shoving the dog into the car trunk.

This time we wouldn't return them.

"Let's just shoot the dogs," Larry said, knowing we had every legal right to kill stray dogs on our land.

"I don't want to start a range war. They might creep up here and do something to get even while we're at work. I don't want to take that chance. Besides, it's not really the dogs' fault . . . it's the owners'!"

"What's your solution?"

"Let's take them to the pound," I said, after we had succeeded in capturing the dogs and locking them in the laundry room. I knew the owner would have to pay a stiff fine to retrieve the dogs. Also, the chances were good the owner wouldn't think of checking a pound sixty miles away.

The next day, and several more times that summer, Larry and I transported hounds to the pound.

By September, Brandy's baby spots were fast disappearing. Unbelievable, but Heidi helped the shedding process by pulling out loose hair, spitting it out, and returning for more. Tiny nubbins also grew as a prelude to the antlers Brandy would exhibit the following year. Brandy was growing up. He ate enough calf manna mate, alfalfa, and browse to satisfy his nutritional requirements, but because he enjoyed the warm milk so much I continued to offer him a bottle twice a day.

"Don't you think Brandy could be weaned now?" Larry asked as I rushed to feed the fawn his bottle before heating TV dinners for us.

"I can't disappoint him."

"It doesn't really matter, as long as you still don't mind getting up early to feed him. I'll fix the dinner if you clean up the mess. I'm starved." That's how Larry started a new habit. His stomach couldn't hold out until I fed deer, raccoons, owl, and fox after waiting all day for food. When Larry became chef, I noticed we more often grabbed a sandwich in town.

Winter generally brought one good snowfall a year to our area. Its clean white beauty was awe-inspiring to me, and Brandy didn't mind it either. Icicles hanging from his whiskers, he still preferred lying in the snow to staying inside the shed.

It was exhausting to feed the livestock and drive to work, but sledding down the hill by moonlight made up for it. Loaded on top of one another, Stephanie, Larry, and I raced the tobaggon down our long pasture hill, as Heidi and Brandy ran beside us. The cool, wet breeze almost froze our bodies as we fell into a snowbank.

One winter the weather was unusually cold, the frost coming suddenly while we were at work. The heavy snowfall made the main highway home nearly impassable.

Our home after a heavy snowfall.

"Shine the flashlight there," Larry yelled, as his frozen hands tried to fasten tire chains. Always prepared for the worst, we carried tire chains in the car throughout the winter. We finally arrived home, two hours later than usual, cold, tried, hungry, and dirty. We remedied everything but the dirt, the water pipes having frozen solid. It wasn't that we weren't clever enough to cover our pipes . . . with a fox in the yard, they didn't stay covered very long. Moreover, our water supply was gravity flow from a spring, so that it was impossible to cover the tubing as far and in as many strange places as the water passed before reaching us. I usually left a faucet running during the coldest time of the year, but it was so cold even that didn't work. At least the livestock had creek water, but it was too far to carry buckets uphill all the way to the trailer just for our use. So for two long weeks we melted snow and went dirty.

But our private ice pond made up for all our inconveniences. Skating on a frozen beaver pond, standing beside a roaring bonfire with a surrounding snow-flocked forest, wild creatures watching us, has to beat even the Ice Capades for beauty. It was still the best winter we'd had.

"Guess what you now have two of?" read the note on the locked driveway gate.

"I brought you another deer," read the second note on the yard gate.

It was a good thing Trooper Stevens left us notes, as there wasn't any sign of another deer. Using flashlights, we spotted a hump under the middle of our mobile home. We waived the beauty of skirting in order to allow Heidi a rather large dry run underneath. At that time of the year, Heidi was usually left inside our home, so Trooper Stevens knew he could leave the new deer in the yard. It was very wild and ran blindly into the fence. Brandy stayed close beside her. Escape cut off, she returned beneath the mobile home. As I crawled on my stomach through the muck, she remained still as I neared. She was in shock, but her eyes finally blinked after I talked quietly to her for an hour. Although she had tried to suck from Brandy earlier, she wasn't interested in the bottle I offered but she did eat several bites of apple and carrots.

One of her eyes was turning white from infection. It was difficult to treat her, wild as she was. I maneuvered her into the fence corner. Then, as she was momentarily distracted by apple bites, I grabbed her neck and put ointment directly into the eye. This small procedure, which had to be repeated twice daily, often took nearly an hour. It meant getting up that much earlier for the morning workout. Larry would have helped, but it frightened her more to have two of us approach her. The eye ointment cured the infection within a few days.

She refused the grain and alfalfa Brandy was willing to share. We picked browse for her, but as soon as her eye cleared up, we felt it best to release her to assure that she would have proper nourishment. As she had never lost her fear of us, she left without a backward glance.

Reluctant to set Brandy free, I must have experienced the pangs of motherhood not uncommon as a baby reaches maturity. But hunting season was over and Brandy was familiar with the ranch from our many walks and horseback rides, so we left the gate to his pen open. He could make his own choice. Heidi still babied Brandy and didn't think he should be free without us. She was very upset, whining and pacing at the fence as she watched him leave.

"Isn't that Heidi and Brandy in the orchard together?" Larry asked as we returned from work the first day Brandy took his freedom.

"No. Heidi never leaves her yard," I answered with confidence.

I didn't know how upset Heidi really was, how desperately she still wanted to look after Brandy, because a closer look did indeed reveal the two of them lying side by side. The woven wire fencing of her yard had been ripped apart so she could join Brandy. Heidi had never done anything like that before. Finally, after the deer had spent many hours alone exploring the surrounding forest while I kept Heidi inside, she accepted the fact that Brandy could get along without her constant surveillance.

"Brandy's sick; he won't take his bottle," I told Larry, after Brandy sniffed the nipple and refused it. Since Brandy was usually frantic for warm pabulum, his strange behavior was worrisome. I watched him closely. Dancing around the back door the next morning, the deer was again anxious for milk. On again, off again, his acceptance-refusal continued for two weeks until he refused the formula altogether. Brandy had weaned himself. About time, too—spring had arrived with a burst of color and a fragrance sweeter than store-bought perfume.

That same spring we nervously awaited the birth of our first calves. Our gray, white, and golden White-face Charlois mixture, mated to the neighbor's Black Angus bull, could produce a colorful calf crop. Larry spent many hours splitting fenceposts and giving them to the neighbor in return for stud fees. We planned to separate each pregnant cow just before parturition so we could handle any complications. Also, brainwashed by farm journals and newspapers, we feared losing a newborn calf to predation and built a calving pen nearby.

"Larry, let's run Queen in; she's due," I announced.

"I checked her udder. She's a few days off yet," he answered smugly. As an Arkansas country boy accustomed to new arrivals, he wouldn't believe me. But, leaving for work the next morning, it was my turn to play smug when we glimpsed a new baby in the far pasture.

We didn't have any better luck with the succeeding cows either. Most of them broke out of our fenced calving pens to find their own laying-in spot as birthing time approached. We searched, but had so much area to cover we rarely found mother and baby until the cow herself was ready to introduce the calf to the herd several days later. Between infrequent nursings, the cow left the calf hidden and returned to the herd alone. So even though our newborn calves were left alone for long periods, where coyotes and bear roam, we lost none to predation. Most calf-predation claims by stockmen are a coverup for inefficient range management practices and could be avoided.

Sheep require close supervision. Sometimes after laying down, they roll over on their side. Their heavy wool then prevents them from getting up again, so they are more vulnerable to predation, but good management practice would still prevent losses without unnecessary slaughter of coyotes.

Numerous devices have been successfully used to frighten away coyotes: flashing warning lights, portable radios left on, even unfamiliar objects with the heavy scent of man will deter them. A new experiment that has proved successful renders sheep distasteful by dousing them with an obnoxious odor, which is repugnant to coyotes. However, we didn't use anything to protect our calves. Too many livestock producers deny that their stock die from poison weeds, inadequate shelter, birth problems, or starvation. It's much easier to condemn the carrion-eating coyote.

We nearly lost a newborn calf another way.

"Did you check the herd?" I asked Larry.

"No. I couldn't find them all. But it's dark now and pouring out. I can't do any more tonight.

"Which cow do I hear bawling?"

"That's Gray One. She can't find her baby. She keeps running from the barn to the orchard. I followed her. I couldn't find her calf either."

"That worries me. Let's go look together."

We followed Gray One to the riverbank. As the mud oozed over my boots, I wished I hadn't been so quick to volunteer. The cow stopped and bellowed louder. If a calf were crying, we couldn't have heard it because of the rushing creek waters.

Larry pointed his flashlight back and forth across the creek bank. "I found it," he yelled.

The freezing water reached the stomach of the frightened

calf, which was standing on a slight ledge in the creek. She was not able to climb out without being swept downstream. Larry inched his way slowly down the bank. He stood in the surging water, then grabbed the calf. Slipping and sliding, he pushed and pulled the ninety-pound calf back to firmer ground.

"Judy, come quick!" he yelled, as Gray One rammed her horns toward him.

I kept between him and the enraged mother. Larry plucked up the calf and ran to the car. We jammed the bawling baby in between us and sped to the barn, where cow and calf were reunited.

The one cow we successfully managed to keep penned in the orchard gave birth right in front of us. To see two, where there was one, is truly awe-inspiring. Watching wide-eyed, Stephanie received answers to several unasked questions.

Sporting names such as Maybelle, Annabelle, Bluebelle, Blackbelle, and Anotherbelle, each baby calf was instantly recognized as a new addition by Brandy, Moab, and the cats, as they sniffed and excitedly licked each one.

Delighted with his freedom, Brandy stayed away more frequently as he became acquainted with wild deer. Not inclined to follow him into the underbrush, Moab stayed home more. Brandy no longer seemed to need the goat's company. Reduced to bawling in the driveway, the disconsolate goat was lonesome and unhappy. He was too large to keep new fawns company the following spring, so we decided to find him a new home.

A lonely female goat, belonging to Miss Knox at Sleepy Hollow Ranch, welcomed him with excited cries. Miss Knox said Moab has also made friends with a wild deer that visits their place. He'll never forget Brandy.

The following summer Trooper Stevens brought us new fawns. A ten-pound male arrived in such perfect condition he had to be named Velvet Prince. We had never seen such a tiny fawn. Even his hooves were still soft. As they harden within a week, we were able to guess his age.

Ignorant interference by people had separated the foundling from his mother; they simply took him from his forest hiding place. A newborn fawn is odorless, and the doe often leaves her baby for long periods to keep her own body scent from giving it away.

Wagging her tail and trembling, Heidi again became a fawn-sitter. Lonely for Brandy, Heidi vibrated with excitement. Velvet Prince welcomed her kisses as she sniffed him all over and performed her cleaning ritual. In the trailer, Velvet Prince jumped on Stephanie's lower bunkbed and decided to call that room home. With a fox and an owl in our bedroom, a raccoon in the yard, and a sea gull in the bathroom, it was as good a place as any. Sleeping most of the time, Velvet Prince proved an easy addition. Stephanie loved the new roommate that shared her pillow.

I started Velvet Prince on goat's milk, because at his young age it offered more nourishment than powdered cow's milk. But at three dollars per twelve-ounce can, it was costing more to feed him than us. I switched him to Brandy's old formula the following month.

A week after Velvet arrived, Trooper Stevens brought another male fawn. This one had been severely injured in a logging accident. It was a wonder he wasn't killed outright by the log that fell on his head. Instead this new fawn had a huge, smelly, infected hole on top of his noggin, and his entire jaw seemed broken, making it nearly impossible for him to eat.

Larry and Trooper Stevens washed the infected wound with surgical soap, then dressed the opening with an antibacterial powder. They also gave him an injection of penicillin to fight the infection. I named the new fawn Baron Duprey, which seemed a dignified name for a fawn that would surely be scarred if he survived.

"He won't eat," I announced to an excited Heidi. Several hours and many attempts later, his crooked mouth was still clenched shut and rejecting the milk because of the pain. Refusing to let him die from starvation, I devoted several days entirely to his care. I enlarged the baby bottle nipple, held the fawn's mouth open, tilted his throat back and squeezed in several drops of goat's milk. Slowly he swallowed. I repeated the process every hour in order not to tire him too much at one time. This routine continued all through the first week. A fawn was surely more important than sleep.

Because the top of Baron Duprey's mouth overlapped the

bottom jaw several inches, we thought the veterinarian should examine him. Riding on my lap during the fifty-mile trip to town, Baron Duprey learned to travel.

"The fracture is too high to do anything about," said the doctor. "It might mend by itself as he grows older. You've done a good job. Just continue the medication."

Baron Duprey sounded like a child's toy horn as he cried in the back room of my office whenever I left him alone to talk insurance. "Oh, that's a patient of mine back there," I explained, proceeding with my sales pitch.

We continued the penicillin injections and wound dressings for two weeks, watching as Baron Duprey miraculously improved. After draining, the wound started to dry up. Still hindered by his crooked jaw, Baron Duprey was at least trying to drink his formula. He had a difficult time sucking the nipple because his mandibles still didn't meet, so as he opened wide I continued to squeeze the goat's milk from the bottle. When Baron Duprey was able to take more formula at a time, I commenced feeding both fawns on the same schedule—five ounces at 6:00 A.M., 6:00 P.M., 10:00 P.M., and 2:00 A.M. Because of my working hours, the feedings were not spread as evenly as they would have preferred, but the fawns thrived on it.

Ever so slightly, as the weeks went by, Baron Duprey's jaw slowly straightened. With this occurrence, I added peeled apple slices, berries, and raisins to the diet. The deer also ate small amounts of browse in Brandy's old pen. Baron Duprey and Velvet Prince were the same age, but the latter matured sooner. His nubbins appeared a month earlier and the dapple fawn spots left his coat a month sooner. Baron Duprey's accident had slowed his growth.

Brandy showed more indifference than curiosity the first time he nosed them through the fence. Having read stories of captive bucks hurting fawns, we didn't let Brandy get any closer. Maturing quickly, Brandy still felt the need to come home every evening for his hour of attention and grain. As his regal antlers grew, he felt too mature to play with Heidi and ignored her efforts to rough-house. He had simply grown up serious and very important.

We received a call from the State Police one midnight to pick up a fawn that had been hit by a car. Calls always come late at

It wasn't unusual for Velvet Prince to join Larry and Stephanie as they played in the creek.

night. . . . or so it seemed. It was 1:30 A.M. when we located the house of the rescuers, forty miles from home.

Dumas must have been a late fawn, because he still had his spots long after those of Velvet Prince and Baron Duprey had disappeared.

"We found the fawn in the middle of the highway, his mother was nudging him to stand, but he couldn't seem to," the young rescuer explained. "We knew he'd be hit again, so we brought him home."

There are occasions when man should interfere, and this was one. Next to hunting, automobiles kill the greatest number of deer. Driving back and forth to work, we see scores every year. We've never hit one because we always slow the car to a crawl when we suspect deer at the roadside. Whenever one is sighted, there are usually more. Most drivers don't realize this. In the spring we always stop by roadside kills to see if the victim is a nursing doe, in which case we search the nearby brush for a fawn.

These young people had already harbored the fawn a full day without giving him nourishment or treatment. His coordination gone, the infant deer was unable to stand without falling.

He held his head completely upside down, and his eyes appeared to focus in opposite directions. He also suffered convulsions every few hours from the time they picked him up.

Before carrying Dumas to the car, Larry gave him a cortisone injection for shock. The fawn survived the journey on Larry's lap. For once we covered the bedroom carpet with canvas and rags before depositing him.

Until Dumas accepted the fact that he couldn't stand up without falling he somersaulted head first, falling into a difficult position unless someone was there to catch him. Larry moved to Stephanie's upper bunk, and I stayed up with Dumas. I couldn't get him interested in warm milk. although he needed the nourishment. Finally he drank from a dish a few sips of warm water with Karo. Clad only in my nightgown, I picked browse by flashlight so he would smell familiar food nearby.

I also cut tiny pieces of apple and pear, opened his clenched jaws, and put the moistened leaves or fruit far back in his mouth. He would then chew, but he wouldn't take food without this help. If I left Dumas alone for more than a few minutes, he would fall on his back unable to right himself, legs extended in the air, eyes rolling. He couldn't even stand to relieve himself, laying in his urine until I moved him. The office remained closed for a day so that I could stay home with him. Dumas required hand feeding in small amounts hourly. Following the veterinarian's telephoned instructions, we gave penicillin, cortisone, and vitamin B injections. The convulsions finally stopped.

The next night Dumas was able to stand for a spell without falling. At first I thought he was just trying his legs, but from 1:00 until 3:00 A.M. he frantically raced around the bedroom in circles. Walking faster and faster, then running, he bumped into walls and padded furniture, fell down, got up, and repeated the mad circling. I couldn't get him to keep still until he exhausted himself completely. I decided this unusual behavior warranted an examination the next day by the veterinarian.

"He seems to have a massive concussion. Just continue the same treatment. I couldn't do any more than you have," Dr. Johnson said.

In my back room at work, Dumas lay exhausted from his

running of the previous evening. He slept the whole time. The only food he swallowed was what I forced into his mouth.

After we rushed home from work, ate, and cleaned up the kitchen, we picked browse, fed all the deer, boiled hypodermic needles, gave injections, fed the raccoons, fox, cats, horses, cows, dog, and treated the latest bird casualty. Then we dropped into bed and merciful unconsciousness. As our wildlife work became better known, the labor increased. So did the veterinary and feed bills. We still had to continue our regular full-time employment to keep everything fed, housed, and well. It was painful to leave Dumas, Baron Duprey, and the others all day . . . then cram a day's worth of care into the hours before bedtime. Nobody complained about the work. We wanted to help. But our daily duties were getting out of hand. We agonized that there must be some way we could devote all our time and effort to the animals.

On Dumas's second morning, at the exact same time—1:00 to 3:00 A.M.—the fawn again underwent an uncontrollable urge to run. It frightened me as he frantically bumped into things, fell down, and got up, only to keep running until he lacked the strength to get up again. I remained awake to offer assistance. During the next several days we continued the injections and hand feeding. Ever so slowly the position of his head returned to normal. By the end of the week the running frenzy had ceased.

Reeking of ordure, even though I changed the rags every time Dumas urinated, the bedroom became unbearable— even for me. I suspected it would also be healthier for Dumas to be in fresh straw bedding that could be changed often. He was now able to walk slowly without falling, and he ate some browse without my assistance. During the two weeks he slept in the bedroom I used only enough heat to remove the chill, so as not to weaken his natural immunities.

We barred Velvet Prince and Baron Duprey from the shed. What I wouldn't have done at that time for the money to build a couple of heated structures! Luckily, Velvet Prince and Baron Duprey were now old enough and well enough to stay outside during the warm summer evenings. Enclosed with fresh straw and no booby traps to fall into, the deer seemed well off. Tootsie, the yellow cat, chose to cuddle near Dumas. Though warm and dry, Dumas developed pneumonia from his weakened condition. The penicillin became ineffective, and he died. We were secure in the knowledge that we had done everything possible for him.

As the days went by, we realized we hadn't seen Brandy lately. It was late summer, too early for mating season to influence him. We searched and called to no avail. Distraction came, however, in the form of a nightmare. Our cattle herd developed a dripping strain of pinkeye.

Ordinarily healthy cows, they contracted the disease from a neighbor's bull, and summer flies had spread the infection immediately. Spraying an antibiotic solution on each eye as they lowered their heads into a bucket of grain was the first futile attempt to overcome the new problem. Treatment had to be administered daily. Result: a bucket-shy herd. It was also too time-consuming. After work, in the short time before dark, it was virtually impossible to locate the herd, move them to the barn, and treat all eyes.

"Judy, if you and Larry will only inject five cc of this into each eyelid, it'll clear up," Dr. Sampson said, handing me a bottle of antibiotic solution. The ordeal of Larry and me wrestling these 1,000-pound animals to inject each eyelid resulted in a physical nightmare quite beyond the comprehension of anyone who has not experienced it.

Almost overnight their eyes turned white. We had no choice. After an exhausting day rebuilding the holding pen, we chased the herd to the barn. Tricking the cows with food, we finally squeezed one into the stall. The trick was to catch the cow's neck as she reached her head through the front slats for grain. Bam! I caught the first one. Pushing with all my strength, I tried to keep her there until Larry could insert boards behind her and run around to secure the next slats.

Larry was the veterinarian and I was the hysterical, unbelieving assistant. "We can't do that. How are we gonna do that? You don't know what you're doing. You'll hit her eye. Let's forget it." Nervous already, Larry reacted negatively to my nagging.

"Shut up and help or leave!" he shouted.

Knowing he would be unable to keep the cow still, hold the eyelid, and give the injection, I kept still and we began working like a team, a very angry team. We did some of our best work without speaking. While I held the cow's head to one side, Larry touched the needle to her eyelid. Before the injection could be accomplished, she yanked her head from my grasp. The project seemed doomed. The cattle would be permanently blinded if we were unable to accomplish the treatment. So, after the fifth try, we gave up being "nice guys."

Larry jammed a nose clamp into the cow's nose and bound it tightly to the barn beam. The metal painfully squeezed her nose if she attempted any movement. As quickly as possible, he injected the shot. There was still an involuntary jump. I patted Larry gently for his steady hand. He understood. Not once throughout the treatment did he make a mistake.

After injecting the antibiotic, applying eye salve, washing faces, and dusting bodies for flies, we released them. Ten cows, nine calves, one bull later, we had it down pat. Larry became a professional. By the time we treated them three weekends in a row, they were cured. Larry dreams of becoming a veterinarian.

In those three weeks that the cattle ran us ragged, we hadn't seen Brandy. Perhaps he had forsaken our friendship to return completely to the wild. He had been so devoted to us, I was sure he wouldn't voluntarily cease visiting the family. I felt the worst had happened: he had been hit by a car or maybe killed by a poacher.

"Find Brandy," I directed Heidi. She would be off, nose to the ground, searching for him. This time intermittent showers had wiped out the deer's scent. Brandy was gone.

As I fed the fawns one evening, a buck came limping toward me from the apple orchard. Alerted, Heidi walked toward him.

"It's not Brandy. It's the wild one we've seen before, Heidi. He'll run off as we get near."

But this time Heidi was right. As the buck came closer, I saw the torn ear. It was Brandy.

"Larry, Brandy's home!" I screamed, throwing my arms around the deer's neck.

After sniffing him, Heidi pulled the matted mud from Brandy's coat and licked him. I hugged and petted the deer as he licked my face. As Larry and I examined him, we discovered what appeared to be a broken hind leg hanging limply. He seemed so skinny. But now that he was home, everything would be remedied. His velvet antlers had really grown in that short time and had begun to branch. Contrary to popular belief, nourishment, not age, is the factor affecting the growth of antlers. Brandy had always eaten better than wild deer.

Limping slowly, Brandy followed us into Heidi's yard. Jenny Raccoon looked down from the huge fir tree as if to say, "What's all the fuss about?"

The break obviously tormented him. He had endured it for possibly three weeks. Unable to get home any sooner, he must have laid up somewhere with his agony. Closer examination revealed that a bullet had broken his leg. A poacher had wounded him. Appraising the situation carefully, we knew Brandy needed more help than we could give. Without considering cost, we sent for the veterinarian.

Dr. Johnson, the doctor who shared patients with Dr. Sampson, was in his first year of practice. It was Sunday, but he drove out as soon as we called. By noon we had begun Brandy's treatment. Dr. Johnson injected a short-acting general anesthetic into Brandy's neck. Not understanding the strange sensation of the drug, Brandy kicked, squirmed, and struggled until he lost consciousness. Completely laid out on the clean grass, Brandy looked dead except for slight breathing.

Working quickly, Dr. Johnson expected Brandy to react the same as a horse and regain consciousness within thirty minutes. After setting the break, he applied a plaster of Paris cast over the entire leg. An hour later, Brandy was still unconscious. Dr. Johnson had to return to town, so after making sure the deer's breathing was normal, he departed, leaving us with instructions. We were worried when hours later Brandy still hadn't moved. Cool dampness replaced the warm sun.

At 8:00 P.M. Brandy's legs started thrashing, his head came up briefly, but he fell back to the ground with a thud.

"Larry, he's coming to. You'd better stay with him," I screamed. Recuperating from the flu, Larry was a poor choice to stand guard in the dampness, but we could not leave Brandy alone. Larry felt better equipped than I to handle the violent thrashings.

We had kept Brandy's tongue moistened during the warm day, but it had still enlarged and dehydrated, making it difficult for him to swallow. Every few minutes Brandy thrashed his legs as he tried to stand. His neck rolled. He simply didn't have the strength to hold it up. Larry held Brandy down, trying to limit the damage the deer could do to himself. Brandy was frantic, not understanding why he couldn't control his legs. The strange cast added to his worry. Suddenly Brandy scooted off around the pasture. It was essential to keep him from tangling in the fence. Larry had a real battle. Brandy wasn't trying intentionally to hurt Larry, but the thrashing of sharp antlers and hooves was a constant threat. Soothed by Larry's voice and petting, the deer voluntarily relaxed a few minutes, then thrashed out again.

It was a night I'm sure Larry would not be anxious to repeat. As I looked out the window to glimpse ailing Larry, handkerchief in hand, sitting on the damp ground with a blanket around his shoulders, I felt more than ever my appreciation for this compassionate man.

Larry never left Brandy's side from 8:00 P.M. until 3:00 A.M., when the deer finally stood without falling. A horse injected with Surital can stand on his own within an hour, so we didn't anticipate such violent drawn-out reactions in a deer. We gave Brandy an injection of medication to help him regain the strength that had ebbed while fighting the effects of the drug. The next morning Brandy was able to limp slowly, dragging the cast behind. Forewarned that sores generally develop in or near the top of a cast, we breathed a sigh of relief when Brandy didn't suffer that added problem. Dr. Johnson had done a good job.

We stood by as Brandy met the fawns for the first time, without benefit of fence between them. As we had only one good deer pen, we were hoping they could share it until Brandy was able to have his cast removed. When the fawns came too near, Brandy stamped his front foot as if to strike at them. That warning was enough to make Velvet Prince and Baron Duprey keep their distance. We weren't worried about Brandy being able to hurt them. He was too weak and awkward in his cast.

After a few days of close confinement with the fawns, Brandy became a paternal figure. He spent hours licking their faces and ears until they shone. Velvet Prince and Baron Duprey thrived on this attention, not to mention that of Heidi who still devoted several hours a day to licking them. Now the fawns had a complete pair of guardians, Brandy and Heidi. Still

Brandy had to wear a cast on his broken leg for several weeks.

drinking their pabulum formula, the fawns also shared choice alfalfa, grain, and all the berries I could pick. It's no wonder I couldn't stand the thought of picking enough berries to make jam.

That summer the fawns were permitted frequent outings to browse and become familiar with their yarding territory, as Brandy had done. Although not restrained in any fashion, the deer preferred sharing their freedom with us.

"I'll race you to the creek," Stephanie shouted, grabbing her swimsuit. As we ran to our swimming hole, Baron Duprey and Velvet Prince bounded along.

Larry was always the first to dive into the creek. After dipping our toes into the icy water, Stephanie and I decided to float on the rubber raft.

"Make Heidi jump out," Larry puffed, attempting to swim while towing us in the raft.

"She won't get out." I lost sight of Larry while hassling with Heidi. "Stop it. I don't want to get wet."

The boat capsized. I screamed. Stephanie giggled. We landed on our heads in the swirling foam.

"You said you wanted to wash your hair," Larry laughed.

A loving armful–Velvet Prince and Baron Duprey. Heidi waits her turn to mother them.

Splash! Baron Duprey leaped into the water, anxious to join the party. Until he was finally panting from exhaustion, he swam proficient laps around us. Velvet Prince and dripping-wet Heidi frolicked on the riverbank. The deer, dog, and we three shared many happy summer days in that ol' swimming hole.

As fall approached, Brandy spent hours beleaguering a tree and rubbing the velvet from his antlers. Surprisingly, he then ate the velvet. Brandy was consistently gentle toward the fawns and us, restricting his sparring to inanimate objects.

The weeks flew by, and before we knew it, the time had come to remove his cast. We couldn't afford to have Dr. Johnson drive this distance again. But he was confident we could handle it ourselves and loaned us the clinic's electric cast cutter. This time Dr. Johnson gave us a different drug to anesthetize Brandy. Larry injected a very small amount. As I held Brandy, he began to drop. We immediately lowered him to the ground. Working furiously, Larry cut each side of the cast and peeled it off within fifteen minutes. Brandy stood without thrashing for thirty minutes, the drug having really made it easier on him.

Brandy was ecstatic to have the burden of the heavy cast removed. He actually pranced and ran back to his pen. The veterinarian suggested we keep him locked up a few more days in order to watch the leg. As deer-hunting season was about to start, we were pleased to have this excuse to protect Brandy from a hunter's gun. The Game Department regulations include even tame deer as targets.

"I've got great news!" Trooper Stevens said, coming by to check Brandy's progress. "Working on a tip, we were searching the logging roads behind you again last night. While I drove the roads, Lieutenant Wilkins set up a roadblock. Sure enough, I saw a suspicious-looking vehicle driving slowly without headlights. When I activated the siren, they stepped on the gas. We slid all over that twisting gravel road. They expected to lose me again. I wish I could have seen their faces when they screamed up to Wilkins' roadblock."

"Are they the ones that have the hounds, too?" I asked.

"Yes. But they didn't have the hounds last night. The one called Skinny said they'd been losing too many good hounds around here lately."

I withheld comment.

"Last night they were spotlighting deer. They had two carcasses with them."

"Are they eating it all or what?" Larry asked.

"No. I could almost understand it if they needed food. But one of them let the cat out of the bag. They've been selling out-of-season venison to restaurants."

"What makes you think they were the same ones that were responsible for our gate?" I asked.

"Same red truck."

"What happens now?"

"They resisted arrest. Caught them red-handed. They'll go to jail. Pay a fine. Even when they get out of jail they won't be allowed to hunt, not for several years. You guys won't be bothered any more."

"Terrific!" All three of us were relieved to know that the confiscated deer carcasses hadn't included Brandy or the fawns. They were still penned up. The enclosure that held them was near an apple orchard where wild deer visit. Every night we shook down apples to share with them. In fact, after our apples were gone we spent lunch hours boxing windfall apples, available for twenty-five cents a box from tree farmers, in order not to disappoint the deer.

During rutting season, Brandy nuzzled a visiting wild doe through the fence. Attacking the tree more furiously in his frustration at not being able to reach her, he looked fearsome. But Brandy continued his tender care of the fawns and was gentle, as always, toward me when I entered the pen. He also continued his close relationship with Heidi. Perhaps pet bucks that have attacked their keepers during rutting season simply did not think of them as part of the family, as Brandy did. He had shared our bedroom too long and our lives too closely to hurt us.

The magic day we released him and the fawns was an occasion for all of us. It was still mating season. Brandy left the fawns to find that doe. Deer exude a strong musk odor from glands on the inside of the hind leg. His nose to the ground, Brandy quickly took off searching for her by this scent. The fawns were still too young to care; hence, they were cautious about accepting freedom too rapidly.

Mother Nature sets a full table in autumn, making it the best time of year to liberate wildlife orphans. Amber the fox was released at the same time as the fawns. Velvet Prince and Baron Duprey were flighty and nervous, unaccustomed to unlimited freedom. Amber crept up behind Baron Duprey, leaped a foot into the air, and yanked a mouthful of white hair from the startled deer's rump. Baron Duprey ran through the orchard, down the driveway, Amber in hot pursuit. Amber's theory was anything that runs should be chased, so like a quick red flame she darted here and there spooking the fawn.

"Amber, stop it!" I yelled, to no avail. "Baron Duprey, come to Mama." I knew he wasn't supposed to understand, but he ran to me for protection anyway. As I held him close, Heidi growled mischievous Amber away from the deer. Amber obeyed.

The fawns were large enough and wouldn't have had anything to fear from a wild fox. But this seven-pound tame tornado sharing the same mother was too close for comfort. The harm could have come from Amber chasing a fawn into the creek or a fence. I caught Amber and locked her up until I could resolve the problem. After thinking about it for the week, my solution was to keep Amber and the fawns together in a fenced area until they became acquainted. I intended to watch and interfere only if the need arose.

The next Saturday I placed Baron Duprey and Velvet Prince in Amber's yard, where they calmly began to nibble the grass. Amber rushed up as if to nip them on the hind leg. The pesty fox put her mouth around the skinny rear leg of Velvet Prince. Heidi whined. I was worried, but Amber didn't bite down. Perhaps she was just testing them. Unable to run far, Velvet Prince whirled around quickly and lowered his head. Bluffable Amber took off. Again, Amber rushed them both, hoping for panic flight. Velvet Prince struck his front hoof at Amber and she retreated again. Now the fawns were braver as they saw the fire leave the flame. Each time a fawn relaxed his guard, Amber launched a sneak attack. But as the frequency picked up, the fawns lost all fear. After several hours of this game of tag, Amber was suddenly "it" and Velvet Prince began chasing her around the yard.

To ensure that their bravery didn't vanish, I continued this treatment for two weekends. The following Saturday, after a week of separation, Amber greeted the fawns happily, sniffing their noses and dancing around them. After the initial play, they paid her no heed at all. We were able to release the fawns and fox so successfully that they often arrived together for nightly visits. Heidi would wait expectantly to examine all her charges.

Hearing a commotion in the orchard one night, I watched Brandy, always recognizable to me by his torn ear, battle another buck. A lump swelled in my throat when I saw Brandy walk off with the waiting doe. Even though Brandy mated, he continued to seek our company every evening. He would

Amber and Baron Duprey become acquainted.

spend several minutes nudging me as I rubbed his neck and hugged him. Heidi nibbled Brandy's fur, and occasionally he rewarded her with a kiss.

Velvet Prince and Baron Duprey remained bachelors the first year. Although no longer fawns, they remained in a group with Brandy and his doe. I often watched Brandy lick their faces and ears in that same paternal way. Velvet Prince and Baron Duprey also craved our companionship. If we were inside the trailer when they wanted attention, they often circled it, bawling for us to come out. "Let me in," Baron Duprey seemed to say, striking the door with his front hoof—and of course I would.

"Let's ride our bikes," one of us would suggest. Velvet Prince and Baron Duprey hearing us pedaling across our gravel lane, would scurry out of the woods to join us. Where we were was where they wanted to be.

We had to be cautious leaving for work in the car. The deer still wanted to follow us. "Honk the horn," I'd tell Larry, at the same time banging noisily against the car door. If they followed us down the highway, it would mean certain death. We successfully alarmed them about cars.

Having read that bucks were loners, I was surprised to

Though living free, all three bucks still considered me mother and often competed for my attention.

observe the interrelationship of our deer toward us and one another. They were extremely sociable, with definite family patterns. In time, Brandy's doe visited with new fawns. She stood afar and nervously watched as Brandy, Velvet Prince, and Baron Duprey touched noses with Heidi and licked my face. Even as mature bucks, during rutting season, the behavior of our three remained unchanged toward us. In the same friendly manner he had as a fawn, Brandy would playfully stand on his hind legs and touch my shoulders with his front legs.

We were humble and proud that our deer trusted us enough to share their freedom with us voluntarily. We could only hope this blind trust and love for us wouldn't be the cause of a bloody death when they encountered the guns of autumn.

SEVEN

Variety Is the Spice of Wildlife

Winning the confidence of a wider circle of people for our work with wildlife was very gratifying, but not without its drawbacks. An even wider variety of animals were being placed with us, but despite the demands on our limited time, the door was always open.

The Eugene Humane Society had given our name to two young men, who were good enough to deliver an elegant animal to my office. This creature had a long body with stubby legs, a pointed muzzle, small ears, and a short tail. About three feet long, he weighed three pounds. His fur was golden, the guard hairs tipped with dark brown, and wore a black band across his eyes. His legs, feet, and tail tip were also black.

"First we named him Arlo the Otter. We even put him in a tub of water, which he didn't like very much," said the young man called John. "Then we thought he might be Willie the Weasel until we read how much smaller weasels are. We finally discovered his identity, and that's why he's now Fairy the Ferret."

They had found this delightful animal running loose in downtown Eugene and, after advertising unsuccessfuully for its owner, decided he should live in a secluded area. Not common to this region, the ferret really shouldn't have been set free.

As he would be a solitary ferret, without any way to reproduce his kind, I opted to release him anyway. Wild ferrets used to be common in the Midwest until the mass poisoning of their staple food, the prairie dog, brought about virtual extinction.

The ferret's distinct musk odor is much stronger than that of a fox. Not merely a scent released in spurts, it is a constantly strong smell that quickly clears congested sinuses. Maybe his owner didn't accidentally lose him after all.

The ferret hated the confining box we placed him in for the long drive home. Tearing the air hole larger, he escaped and completed the journey quietly on Larry's lap. We kept him inside with us the first night, intending to make a temporary feeding place for him in the old ranch house. Fairy completely ignored the kitty litter box. Just after I decided he wasn't housebroken, he used the commode water.

Fairy wasn't afraid of Heidi. He lay quite still as she excitedly rolled him on his back and kissed his stomach. Fairy was very friendly, jumping at my feet or chasing after me. He tried to coax me into playing with him. Stephanie enjoyed tug-of-war with this frisky but quiet visitor. Habitually behind the sofa, on his back with his nose touching his tail, he slept.

After reading several books on ferrets, I felt sure that this specimen would be able to fend for himself and revert easily to the wild. We released him at the old house, supplying the dry dog food diet until he didn't require it any more. Living a free life, Fairy didn't need our companionship. We didn't see him again until two years later when Larry took a picture of him venturing out from under the old house.

One afternoon a possum entered the picture when a stranger called my office. Momentarily confused by the "Hughes Insurance" telephone response, she went on to ask, "Would you take a possum I just found?"

The only North American marsupial, the opossum is completely helpless at birth—blind, deaf, and so small that two dozen could fit onto a teaspoon. Because her young are born in such an undeveloped stage, the mother has to carry them in an abdominal pouch for several weeks. Newborn opossums, without help from their mother, must find the pouch where milk, warmth, and security await them. Many don't make it.

Eyes still closed and looking more like a tiny rat, the opossum foundling brought to me was the smallest I had ever seen.

"I found the mother and other babies dead. I looked in the mother's pouch and found this one still alive," the woman said.

Placing the opossum on cotton in a small container, I rushed next door to the market for condensed milk. He took several

Fairy the ferret.

drops from a tiny pointed eye dropper. His little forelegs reached out as if to hold the glass tube as he swallowed the life-sustaining liquid. However, already infested with maggots, he was extremely weak, having been without nourishment too long. He died a few hours later.

We took in another opossum that had a much better chance for survival. Fluffy except for his hairless tail and ears, he seemed to be mostly eyes. Although young, he was well developed. A boy had found the possum family under his house and had grabbed a baby from its mother's back, with the intentions of keeping it as a pet. After a few days, he decided it was "too primitive" and called us.

Larry and I temporarily consigned the opossum to a cage, where he willingly ate dry dog food, apples, and grapes. Even though he was accustomed to being held, the opossum evidenced extreme nervousness. He growled, exposing a well-constructed set of sharp teeth. He wasn't frightened enough to "play possum," the semi-rigid catatonic state of make-believe death for which the animal is famous. In this state, even the heartbeat and respiration diminish, the tongue hangs out, and the eyes film over.

When we thought the opossum was old enough, we opened

the cage door. He returned several times for food, and then made his final solitary foray into the woods.

More than any other species, skunks carry the greatest threat of transmitting rabies to people, even being capable of passing on the disease when they don't actually have it themselves.

"I wouldn't touch them with a ten-foot pole," a local veterinarian had warned me. "And I've had a rabies preventative shot."

"The odds are a million to one against them carrying rabies. Only three people in the United States have died from rabies in the last ten years," a second veterinarian advised.

Deciding to abide by that opinion, I accepted three striped skunk orphans which had been found near the body of their mother, victim of a "hit and run" accident.

"Look at the fleas!"

Because of their tender age, which I judged at approximately six weeks, I hestitated using flea powder, but it was obvious that the fleas created an immediate threat to the skunks' survival. I shook cat flea powder across their necks. Within an hour the floor was littered with dead flea bodies.

Not wanting intentionally to tame the skunks, I didn't handle them unnecessarily. We could distinguish them by a slight discrepancy in their white markings. I overcame my urge to name one Flower and instead called them Chanel #5, 6, and 7. In order to feed them several times a day, I carted them back and forth to work with me. They wouldn't suck a doll bottle and were too inept at drinking from a dish, so I slowly offered milk, egg yolk, and Karo syrup with a syringe. Their long claws held the syringe as they gobbled several cubic centimeters several times a day.

For the first few days, they were content to eat and sleep in a small cage. But, as their strength increased, I moved them to a larger outdoor pen. They also graduated to canned and dry dog food with their milk treat. They made their mess in a cat litter box, so they were very easy to keep clean.

Every evening I carried them to a new part of the woods. They sniffed, explored, and grubbed around the exciting forest while I watched them. Heidi whined and fretted. "Why can't I help?" she seemed to whimper. I felt in the wild the skunks would be at a disadvantage if they forfeited their natural fear of dogs. They might hesitate too long before secreting their protective odor.

Even though the skunks recognized me as "mother," any sudden move caused a threatening erect tail and foot stamping. They never sprayed me . . . just capricious bluffers.

The three males enjoyed a close brotherly relationship. They tumbled, jumped, and chewed one another, to an accompaniment of growls and howls. How did I know? Their cage was right outside our open bedroom window. The skunks' favorite game was to bob back and forth toward one another. They bounced both hind feet in the air, then threw their tails up, threatening to fumigate. It was all in fun and they never sprayed one another.

As the skunks became more adept and worldly wise, I left their cage door open. At first they played in the hay, searched the garbage, and explored the woodpile. Strange noises sent them scurrying for cover. They usually returned home by midnight. I couldn't sleep until I had them safely locked back in their pen.

"Let's watch the fireworks," I said, as skunk and raccoon met for the first time at the feeding station.

Briefly touching noses, the raccoon and skunk hastened in opposite directions. No turmoil at all.

After several evenings of unlimited freedom, the skunks were no longer anxious to return to home base.

"You know I can't sleep until I have all of them," I explained to Larry, who was patiently waiting for me to join him in bed.

"Heidi, find the baby," I directed, flashlight in hand. Although she had been kept away from the skunks, Heidi knew that command.

Under the woodpile, behind the barn, through the woods, we tracked them. Suddenly Heidi thrust her nose into a pile of brush. While focusing the light on Channel #5, I reached for the little stinker. Heidi thought she deserved a fast lick as reward for locating the skunk. She slobbered on him just as I picked him up. Chanel #5 raised his tail and shot a stream of fragrant juice toward her, enveloping us. It wasn't as potent as an adult skunk's odor and evaporated rapidly. After Heidi's face was washed with tomato juice, she regained her doggy

Handfeeding Chanel #5.

smell. I was delighted to know they were capable of defending themselves in true skunk fashion. As the maturing skunks foraged for their own mealworms, bugs, berries, and apples, they gradually became independent.

"It's only a robin." How often we take this popular bird for granted. Until I met Polo, I was guilty of the same oversight.

Polo had fallen from the safety of her nest to the chaos of a downtown trailer court. Dogs and cats ran free. Bicycling children screamed for attention. It was no place for a grounded nestling. If a cat didn't kill it, the night temperature would. It was also a frustrating experience for the mother robin. Unable to save her offspring, she scolded and shrieked as I scooped the nestling into a bed of Kleenex to take home.

Inside our heated bathroom, Polo kept very snug. She sat in a margarine dish covered with a handkerchief. Dipping my finger into a fine mash of hard-boiled egg yolk and milk, I stuck it in Polo's gaping mouth. She ate willingly. Many people mistakenly drown baby birds by forcing water down them. Nestlings don't require water until they mature. During daylight hours, baby birds must eat every few minutes, so Polo became my constant companion. Chirp! chirp! signaled my ravenous eater.

This robin was no bird brain. Even as a completely helpless ball of fluff, she didn't soil her nest. When she had to mess, Polo stood up, inched her way backward, and aimed it over the rim. In my experience, all baby birds will do this if their nest is situated high enough in a box.

Within her first week, Polo had graduated from the nest box to roosting on a wooden rod inside a large parakeet cage. In no time at all she could fly between the perches.

"Chop it up," I instructed Larry, as he tantalized Polo with a two-inch mealworm. Gulp! Polo gobbled it whole with gusto. I also added to her diet bits of apple, orange, peach, grapes, and berries. Polo thrived.

As she grew, Polo had unlimited freedom in my office, and at home the bathroom was her private domain. She generally sat on the shower rod, thus messing in the tub, which was easy to clean. As she practiced flying in my office, Polo's determination was visible as she perched on the edge of her cage, flapping her wings. Plop! Another forced landing. After several attempts, the little robin flew several feet to my lap. It was her twelfth day as my guest.

"When are you going to let Polo fly outside?" Larry asked.

"Certainly not yet. She's still too young. I don't want her to fly away before she's capable of sustaining herself."

"I think you're making a mistake. If you give her freedom

Polo the clever robin.

now, while she still regards you as her mother, she's more likely to get used to her liberty by degrees. Then it won't be such a big deal later. If you wait, for sure she'll take off."

"Okay." I reluctantly agreed to turn Polo loose on the lawn.

The little robin scurried around the yard, nibbling at minute bugs. As I dug up a fresh worm, Polo excitedly bobbed her head back and forth, grabbed one end, and pulled the worm out by herself. Polo really delighted in the warmth of the June sun. Putting her tummy to the ground, she gently dusted her outstretched wings in the dirt.

Polo didn't attempt flight at all. After a few more minutes, I snatched her back to the safety of the bathroom. "More next weekend," I promised.

Next Saturday, somewhat calmer about releasing her, I placed Polo on the branch of an apple tree. She surveyed the entire area from that branch for two hours and then suddenly took flight.

"Polo, Polo," I called, upset by her disappearing act. "Chirp! Chirp!" She answered in her easily recognizable voice.

"There she is," I pointed a hundred feet away. "In that fir tree."

We were proud of her fancy flight work. All day, Larry, Stephanie, and I took turns scanning the treetops for Polo. She stayed well out of reach, flitting from tree to tree, though she did remain in the general area. Heidi was also aware of Polo's unique chirp. She often spotted the robin before I did and then stationed herself beneath the tree, looking upward and whining.

Polo continued to mimic our calls as she busily partook of the banquet of bugs the tall timber had to offer. As evening approached, I began to worry about leaving her out overnight.

"Polo, Polo!" Swoosh. She answered by landing nearby. After she let me catch her, I squired Polo back to the bathroom for the night.

"Are you going to turn her loose again tomorrow?" Larry asked.

"Well . . . no. We won't be here."

"I think she should start developing her natural ability now. We'll be home early this week. I think you should."

I gave in and the cats were permanently locked inside. I liberated Polo with a full stomach and placed water and pieces of fruit high on hay piles inside the barn.

"Will Polo be waiting when we get home?" We were all anxious on the drive home. I felt a stir on my shoulder as soon as I climbed out of the car. "She's still here!" As I shoveled an area we had kept moistened for worms, Polo flew to the ground, listening. An apt pupil, she spied dinner before I did.

Again, I put her inside before dark, although I continued her daily freedom. Every afternoon Polo greeted our return. She ignored the wild robins. Indeed, when she viewed her reflection in the bathroom mirror, she savagely attacked it. Did she expect to look like the rest of the family?

Polo was quickly becoming adept at finding her own food, although she was lazy, preferring to hold open a gaping mouth for me to fill. She often caught bugs, worms, and once devoured a bee right in front of me.

When we were home, Polo craved our companionship. She sat on the porch, above the door, or near a window, chirping for us to join her. In her anxiety to be with us, she once flew into the dining-room window. When we were outside, she tagged along. We always had to watch where we walked, as Polo now spent more time on the ground racing behind us than in the trees.

While Polo was with us, we were also caring for an injured woodpecker. Polo watched as I sat the newcomer on a nest of ants. As the flicker devoured ant eggs, Polo scampered over and gave him a swift zap on the head. I had to pull her off the weak woodpecker. Was Polo jealous?

Polo loved taking baths. If her dish of water was empty, she perched on the outdoor faucet and squawked until I refilled it. Showers were also welcomed . . . whenever the sprinkler flowed, she would be absorbing droplets of water. She had a habit of soaking herself so thoroughly that she couldn't fly for several minutes. While we were at work, I made sure her bathing dish was high off the ground.

Polo was growing up, time for her to begin staying outside at night. She had to learn to tolerate outside temperatures during the summer months so she could survive the winter. One warm evening I filled her plump stomach even fuller and left her out. I fretted. Would she know enough to roost all night? At sunrise Polo was at Stephanie's window screaming for a breakfast handout.

By the end of July, Polo was a totally liberated robin, although she still desired our company. She would fluff out in my lap, totally relaxed for hours at a time. Toward late August, Polo became more self-reliant. She no longer slighted neighborhood robins. She still wanted my company, but not as frequently. At the end of the month my mother became resident caretaker when we had to be away for several weeks. Polo evidently viewed Mom as a stranger, because she would not accept handouts directly from her. No longer finding us at home, Polo discontinued her visits.

"Polo! Polo!" I pleaded, as soon as we returned from our sojourn. One little robin flew closer and perched above me, uttered one last cheep, then joined another. I'd like to think Polo said goodbye.

One year in the middle of winter we made a home for an injured sparrow hawk, so ill we were certain it would die. Both wings and legs were immobile. The sparrow hawk is the smallest member of the falcon family in the Western Hemisphere. It eats insects, mice, and very small birds.

The day our frightened sparrow hawk arrived, we placed her in a warm box and left her alone in the living room until she calmed down. I fed her the same diet I had given Spook, the screech owl, chicken liver and hearts dipped in dried egg shell. As the little hawk was in no mood to eat, I held her in my left hand and gently opened her beak, forcing the food down.

During the first few days her condition seemed to worsen. When she tried to fly, she fell. Her legs were useless. Then I increased the dosage of Cosa Terramycin, coating her food with it every time I fed her. Suddenly, after several days on the drug, she flew and used both legs.

Setting her free in the orchard, we happily watched as she spiraled higher and higher. While soaring, she saw a worm on the ground and was able to stoop and close with it. Because her chances of recovery had seemed so slim, her phenomenal progress overjoyed us both.

As Larry walked in the woods one day, he found a colorful western tanager with a broken wing. From the red head, yellow breast, and black back, we identified it as a male. Once inside a bird cage, he ate oranges, grapes, corn flakes, apples, and bird gravel.

Waiting for his wing to heal, he seemed lonely, so I moved his cage near Sunny, our parakeet, and put a mirror in with him, which seemed to improve his disposition. We allowed the tanager to fly in the living room with the parakeet, but they

The sparrowhawk.

ignored each other. During warm summer days we transferred the tanager to a large outdoor cage, where he could begin to exercise his wing as he felt stronger.

In time the wing healed. The cage door was left open and he took off quickly.

After examining a bird found in the park, Dr. Tripp, a veterinarian two towns away, called me.

"He has a bruised wing and leg, but I can't find anything else wrong. You can probably turn it loose in a few days," he told me.

I drove thirty miles to pick up the killdeer. It was easy to identify because of the white breast with two black bands, pointed beak, and long legs.

Knowing the species to be an insectivore, I offered canned dog food, which he gulped with great gusto. Good, I wouldn't be confronted with the usual bird problem of force feeding. The warm summer days made it possible for him to remain in the large outdoor cage. As I knew he didn't have internal injuries, my plan was to release him after allowing time for the bruises to heal. Whenever a cat walked by the cage, he uttered a sharp piercing call. Strangely enough, when the dog walked by, it didn't affect him at all.

On a beautiful clear day, I opened the cage door (after locking up the cats). The killdeer flew perfectly. Circling back and landing nearby in the driveway, he gave a shrill cry and took off again. He stayed nearby and repeated this several times during the day. Like all our wildlings, large and small, his return to good health was a cause for rejoicing, tinged of course with regret when he took off for good.

As a mature buck, Brandy remained devoted to Stephanie.

EIGHT

Promises to Keep

Showing a creek to a raccoon for the first time, salvaging a wounded owl . . . bountiful compensation for us. Unfortunately, that didn't satisfy the creditors. Never mind *keeping up* with inflation, we were dropping further behind.

I don't remember when our whispered discussions about selling the ranch changed from 'should we' to '*when* should we.' Maybe it was the months of the gasoline crisis . . . the wasted hours spent waiting in line to pay exorbitant prices for gas we needed to commute fifty-five miles. The price of fuel had doubled since we moved to the ranch. Maybe it was the month we couldn't pay the veterinarian . . or the fact that the feed bill had tripled since we inaugurated our wildlife hostel. Or perhaps it was the day of the storm that took our barn and cages. We knew we couldn't replace either. Possibly it was the day we had to change cars again. Three cars in four years . . . the last one wasn't even paid for when a rod blew through the engine.

As we tightened our belts, we knew we would never sell to just anyone. A developer had approached us about subdividing the ranch and selling the parcels for enough to ease our old age. But a dollar sign had never been the important thing to us. If we could have made it, we would have been content to live there forever. If we couldn't, we certainly wouldn't plunder it by allowing hordes of people to disrupt the wildlife. But could we find someone who would appreciate the ranch as much as we did?

We were interested in selling the ranch only to conservationists. With that in mind, we informed only certain nature magazines and organizations of our intention to sell. A television personality wrote to us requesting information about our ranch. When could he come see it?

"How will we possibly entertain a 'Hollywood couple' for a week?" I nervously asked Larry. "What will we talk about? Where will we put them? What will we feed them? What will they expect? From viewing the debonair film roles he played, I expected a well-dressed snob. How could he possibly appreciate the ranch?

They came. Mr. X bounded from the car wearing jeans and a sweatshirt. When I read the stickers plastered on his car, Wear Fake Fur, I Don't Hunt, Animals Have Rights, Arm Bears, my anxiety melted away. Here was a kindred spirit.

"You can use Stephanie's room during your stay," I offered.

"No, thanks. We'll just sleep out here in our sleeping bags," he answered.

"Let's take a look at the ranch," I suggested for the first of many hours spent trekking the property. We walked and talked.

"We want it!" they decided.

It was done. Bear Creek Ranch was no longer ours.

The new owners didn't continue our wildlife halfway house, however, they did employ full-time caretakers to keep trespassers and hunters away from the property.

Of course we feel sad, viewing a picture of Heidi licking Brandy or Stephanie cuddling Amber. But the animals were never meant to be 'ours'. We wanted them to live as normally as possible. To that end, we are satisfied with our achievements.

Though separated from the ranch, Larry, Stephanie, Heidi, the horses, cats and I continue to live in the country. We are still very much involved with helping wildlife. Currently, two barn owls are convalescing in our bathroom and a raccoon temporarily resides in the pantry.

We keep track of important legislation and decisions affecting animals. We try to speak for those who can't. Unfortunately, defending wildlife is a never-ending task. It requires those of us who care to become actively involved in promoting their cause.

On a personal level, Larry and I are working diligently toward our goal of re-creating and expanding our wildlife hostel elsewhere and hope to some day acquire enough wilderness property to insure a protected buffer zone for orphaned and injured wildlings. We are eagerly anticipating the time we will host a fawn on the pillow once more.